IELTS *Practice Now*

Practice in Listening, Reading, Writing and Speaking
for the IELTS Test

by

Carol Gibson, Wanda Rusek and Anne Swan

C ▴ A ▴ L ▴ U ▴ S ▴ A

Centre for Applied Linguistics in the University of South Australia

CALUSA
82–98 Wakefield Street
Adelaide SA 5000

University of South Australia
North Terrace
Adelaide SA 5000

First published 1996
Second printing (with amendments) 1996

Copyright © 1996
School of Language and Literacy Education, University of South Australia

ISBN 0 86803 142 9

ACKNOWLEDGEMENTS

The authors and publisher would like to express their gratitude to Stephen Slater their editor and to Frank Packenham for page layout, typesetting, visuals and editing assistance. Thanks to: all teachers and students at CALUSA who helped to trial the test practice materials, in particular Steve Cook, Joan Tobella and Barbara Reichert; to the students of ELP, Universitas Islam Indonesia for their assistance with trialling materials; the following people for their assistance with the recording of Listening and Speaking Test material—Pehr Abrahamsson, Kirill Pogorelov, Maria Mahamood, Rachael Kirkham, Rosemary Pimlott, Peter Forward, Alison Banks, Mandy Rego, Graham Ross, Neil Low, Peter Cowling and Shane McCarthy. Finally, thanks to copyright owners for permission to reproduce copyright material.

Cover design by Caroline Rannersberger.
Line drawings on pages 18, 19, 24, 29, 31, 32 by Midori Nakamura and page 93 by Peter Forward.
OzArt clip art and Australian Heritage Illustrations by New Horizons.
Set in Palatino using PageMaker 6.0.
Printed by Document Services, University of South Australia.

Contents

Themes – Reading Tests

The marginal page markers: 39, 49, 59, 68, 78, 87, 96, 104, 111

Themes – Writing Tests

The IELTS Test

IELTS means International English Language Testing System. It is an internationally accepted English language test which assesses whether or not your English language skills are strong enough to commence studying at a university or at a vocational college in an English speaking country.
Over 40,000 candidates sit for the IELTS test worldwide every year.

The IELTS test is not a test which you can pass or fail. IELTS tells you something about your English language weaknesses and strengths.

There are 4 subtests—Listening, Reading, Writing and Speaking.
Your result from each of these subtests is given individually on a scale from 1–9 and then all 4 scores are averaged to give the Overall Band Score.

An outline of each Overall Band Score is given below.

9 **Expert User.** Has fully operational command of the language: appropriate, accurate and fluent with complete understanding.

8 **Very Good User.** Has fully operational command of the language with only occasional unsystematic inaccuracies and inappropriacies. Misunderstandings may occur in unfamiliar situations. Handles complex detailed argumentation well.

7 **Good User.** Has operational command of the language, though with occasional inaccuracies, inappropriacies and misunderstandings in some situations. Generally handles complex language well and understands detailed reasoning.

6 **Competent User.** Has generally effective command of the language despite some inaccuracies, inappropriacies and misunderstandings. Can use and understand fairly complex language, particularly in familiar situations.

5 **Modest User.** Has partial command of the language, coping with overall meaning in most situations, though is likely to make many mistakes. Should be able to handle basic communication in own field.

4 **Limited User.** Basic competence is limited to familiar situations. Has frequent problems in understanding and expression. Is not able to use complex language.

3 **Extremely Limited User.** Conveys and understands only general meaning in very familiar situations. Frequent breakdowns in communication occur.

2 **Intermittent User.** No real communication is possible except for the most basic information using isolated words or short formulae in familiar situations and to meet immediate needs. Has great difficulty understanding spoken and written English.

1 **Non User.** Essentially has no ability to use the language beyond possibly a few isolated words.

When you decide that you would like to do further study in an English speaking country, the university or college you apply to will say what minimum score you will need in order to enrol in the course of study you have chosen. This score will probably be between 5.5 and 7.0. Some universities also require a minimum bandscore on a particular subtest, such as Writing or Speaking.

The Listening and Speaking subtests focus on general English.

The Reading and Writing subtests are more closely related in content to academic styles of English.

The subtests are always taken in the following order:

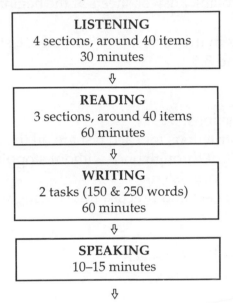

Total Test Time: 2 hours 45 minutes

Questions most often asked about the IELTS test

Do I have to do all 4 sections of the test?
Yes you do. The Overall score is calculated as an average of all 4 subtests.

If I don't get the score I need, can I do the test again?
You will have to wait 3 months before you can do another test.

How soon can I get my results?
Most IELTS test centres can give you your results within 1 week.

For further information about the IELTS test, you can refer to *The IELTS Handbook,* which is available at the nearest IELTS test centre.

Using this Book

To the student

These 3 complete Listening tests, 9 complete Reading tests, 9 complete Writing tests and 2 Speaking tests, have been prepared so that you can practise on your own or in a classroom with the help of a teacher. They have been trialled with students at different levels and at language centres internationally. Feedback from trialling has been incorporated at each stage of development.

Procedure for Listening, Reading and Writing Tests

Do these practice tests under strict test conditions.

Time yourself carefully and **do not use a dictionary**.

You may photocopy the blank answer sheets at the beginning of each test section or use your own paper.

You can practise the tests in the correct order or select tests according to thematic interest, using pages 2 and 3.

Listening tests

In each test there are 4 sections.

- All dialogues and instructions for each test are on the audio tape, cassette 1.
- Play the audio tape right through once without stopping.
- Write your answers as you listen.
- Photcopy the answer sheet and practise transferring your answers onto it.

Reading tests

In each test there are 3 reading passages.

- Read the instructions carefully.
- Start at the beginning.
- Follow the suggested time for each set of questions.
- Photcopy the answer sheet and write your answers directly onto it.

Writing tests

In each test there are 2 tasks.

- Read the questions carefully.
- Answer both tasks.
- Follow the suggested time and length for each task.

Procedure for Speaking Tests

- Work through the exercises using the audio tape, cassette 2.
- Use the transcripts at the end if you want to listen to and read the interviews.
- Practise with a partner if you can.

This symbol appears in various places. It is there to remind you to carry out one or more of the following activities after you have finished a task or a test.

- Check your answers to the Listening, Reading and Speaking tests using the Answer key at the back of the book.
- Rate your performance on the Writing tasks using the Self-Rating Guide on pages 135 and 136.
- Carry out the Reflection tasks at the end of each subtest section.

To the teacher

If the IELTS test is new to you, you will find the introductory description of the test on pages 4 and 5 useful. You will probably also wish to go through that section with your students to forestall some of their queries. If your students have not done the IELTS Test before you may find it helpful to go through a test, section by section in class, discussing the question types at some length. You may also wish to draw your students' attention to the Hints and Reflections for each subtest and discuss them further as you think necessary. Here are some quick hints for you to follow as you prepare your students for the test using *IELTS Practice Now*.

Listening Tests

- Work through one section at a time before doing a full test.
- Do under test conditions so that students get used to hearing the material once only.
- Give students practice in transferring their answers to separate sheets of paper as required in the real test.
- Go over the answers with your class, playing the tape again to clarify any difficult questions.
- Discuss strategies – How to use the time given to scan questions.
  – What to do if a question is missed or not understood.

Reading Tests

- Use Themes—Reading Tests, page 2, for guidance as to the content of the reading tests, in case you wish to concentrate on a particular theme.
- Work through one section at a time, pointing out the different question types, before doing a full test. Focus on the question types your students find difficult.

Writing Tests

- Set as homework tasks or do in the classroom under strict test conditions.
- Give the students timed practice to help them organise themselves under test conditions.
- Do follow-up work on the particular aspects of writing you feel need developing, such as understanding and answering the question, developing an argument, using appropriate register, improving sentence structure, or any other skills normally required for academic writing.

Speaking Tests

- Do the exercises individually or in small groups.
- Give students opportunities to practise all four phases
- Remember that your role as mock examiner will be important here in providing authentic practice and relieving the stress that this subtest tends to cause.
- Help students to develop expressions which are useful when handling hesitation or misunderstanding.
- Use the transcripts to point out any features of conversational ability that demonstrate a candidate is comfortable with English in an interview situation.

Help the students understand that the skills required are useful, not just for the test, but for reading and writing in academic contexts and for listening to and speaking with native speakers.

HELPFUL HINTS
Hints for Test Day

 Eat a healthy breakfast.

Drink water.

 Arrive at least half an hour before the test starts so you can remain calm.

Don't panic.
Panic makes you lose concentration.

Make sure you know when and where your speaking test is.

Room 29

DO NOT DISTURB

IELTS
Speaking Test
in progress

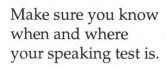 Make sure you know your candidate number.  **768**

Listen carefully to all the instructions.

If the room is too noisy, tell the teacher.

If you can't hear the tape clearly in the listening test, tell the teacher.

 During the break between the reading and writing tests, leave the room, have a drink of water and walk around.

Hints for the Listening Test

Questions

Hints

What if I can't hear the tape very well?

You should tell the teacher immediately.

Where do I write my answers?

Write them in the question booklet. At the end of the test transfer your answers to the answer sheet.

Should I answer the questions as I listen?

Yes. Don't wait till the end of the section because you'll forget the answers.

What if I miss a question?

Don't panic. Keep going. You may have a chance to go back to do it later.

Can I look at the questions before I hear the dialogues?

There's time before each section for you to look ahead at the questions .

Is there time to check my answers?

There's time to check your answers at the end of each section and at the end of the whole test.

Hints for the Reading Test

Questions   **Hints**

What is the best way to do the reading sections?

First, read the questions for each section and then, read the reading passages.

Can I write the answers in the question booklet?

No. Write your answers directly onto the answer sheet.

How can I use time wisely?

Answer questions in their order and check the time regularly.

What if I can't answer some questions?

Leave the ones you can't answer and do those you can. If you have time at the end, try the ones you left.

Hints for the Writing Test

Questions

Hints

Should I do Writing Task 1 before Writing Task 2?

Answer the task you feel most confident about first. If Task 1 looks easier than Task 2, do that first.

My spelling is weak. Will my spelling mistakes ruin my score?

A few spelling mistakes should not affect your score.

What if I don't keep to the recommended times?

The time lines are suggestions only but it's wise to spend 20 minutes on Task 1 and 40 minutes on Task 2, since Task 2 is worth more than Task 1.

Is it OK to write in pencil?

Pencil is allowed but make sure it is dark enough to be easily read by the assessor.

Hints for the Speaking Test

Questions

Hints

How can I prepare myself for the speaking interview?

Practise speaking as much English as possible in a relaxed and friendly way. Don't rehearse!

What should I do if I don't understand the interviewer?

Ask the interviewer to repeat the question. Don't panic.

What if I can't think of anything to say straightaway?

Ask the interviewer to give you a few moments to think.

Is it better to speak accurately?

The best speaking is a natural conversation. Smile and enjoy yourself.

What if my pronunciation is not very good?

Try to give your voice variety of tone to show that you are lively and interested.

LISTENING PRACTICE TESTS

There are 3 listening practice tests

Time allowed for each test: 30 minutes

Before you start
All the dialogues and instructions for each test are on the audio tape.
When you are ready to begin the test, start the tape.
DO NOT STOP THE TAPE BEFORE THE TEST IS FINISHED.
Photocopy the answer sheet on the next page and practise transferring your answers onto it.
When you have finished each test, check your answers with the answer key on page 177.

LISTENING ANSWER SHEET

Photocopy this page to write your answers to each Listening test you practise.

Test number:

Enter the number in the boxes and shade the number in the grid.

| 00 | 10 | 20 | 30 | 40 | 50 | 60 | 70 | 80 | 90 |

↑ ↓

| 0 | 1 | 2 | 3 | 4 | 5 | 6 | 7 | 8 | 9 |

1	
2	
3	
4	
5	
6	
7	
8	
9	
10	
11	
12	
13	
14	
15	
16	
17	
18	
19	
20	
21	
22	
23	
24	
25	

26	
27	
28	
29	
30	
31	
32	
33	
34	
35	
36	
37	
38	
39	
40	

| Band Score | | Listening Total | |

LISTENING TEST 1

SECTION 1

Questions 1–9

Questions 1–4

Write your answers in the spaces provided.

> *Example:*
>
> > COMPUTER
> >
> > *Room B100*

1.

> _____
>
> COMPUTERS IN
>
> THIS ROOM

2.

> COMPUTERS FOR
>
> _____
>
> USE ONLY

3.

> MAXIMUM TIME
>
> FOR EACH BOOKING
>
> _____

4.

```
┌─────────────────────────────────┐
│         OPENING TIMES           │
│                                 │
│   MON–FRI _____      │
│                                 │
│   SAT–SUN _____      │
│                                 │
└─────────────────────────────────┘
```

Questions 5–9

Complete the following statements as briefly as possible.

5.   To obtain paper for printing insert _____ .

6.   Automatic _____ checks for computer virus.

7.   Barbara's student number is _____ .

8.   To book a computer, students have to write their _____

     and _____ in the book.

9.   No _____ or _____ in the computer

     room.

SECTION 2

Questions 10–16

Circle the correct letter.

Example:	Barbara and Ricardo have
	A passed their exams (B) finished their exams
	C finished their course D failed their exams

10. *Circle the correct letter.*

How much will it cost each person for the riverboat trip?

A $30

B $20

C $25

D $5

11. *Circle **TWO** correct letters.*

Indicate the **TWO** reasons why Barbara and Ricardo decide **NOT** to go horseriding.

A   it's too expensive

B   they haven't got the right equipment

C   it's too far away

D   Ricardo can't ride a horse

E   they don't want to catch a bus

12. *Circle the correct letter.*

How much was quoted in the brochure for the hire of a mountain bike?

A $20 per day + $10 deposit

B $10 per day + $20 deposit

C $30 per day + $10 deposit

D $30 per day + $20 deposit

13. *Circle the correct letter.*

Where is the bicycle hire place?

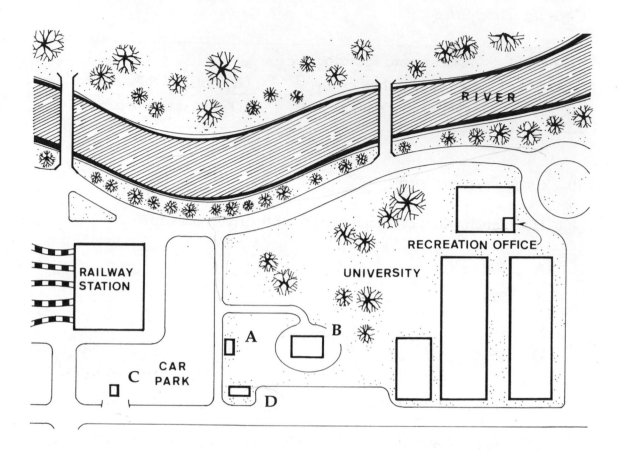

14. *Circle the correct letter.*

What is included in the hire charge?

A   helmet, panniers and lights

B   panniers and repair kit

C   helmet and repair kit

D   repair kit, helmet and lights

15. *Circle the correct letter.*

What did Barbara and Ricardo hire?

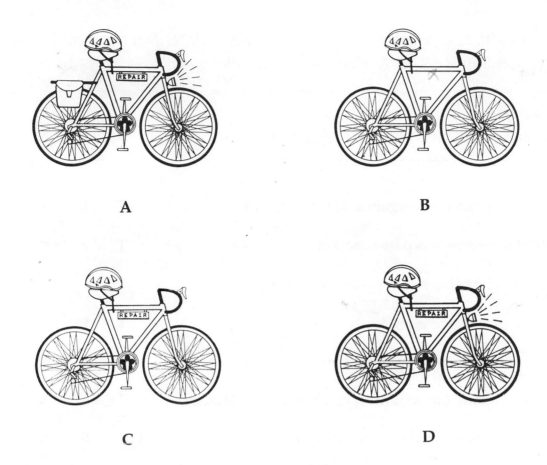

A

B

C

D

16. *On the receipt below, write in the correct total amount paid by Barbara and Ricardo.*

Receipt for Bicycle Hire

Amount received:

$ _____

Date: ___ 6 June ___

SECTION 3

Questions 17–23

*Look at the statements numbered 17–23. As you listen, circle **T** if the statement is true,
F if the statement is false or **N** if there is no information given.*

Example:			
All students have to write an assignment	T	F	(N)

17. Work experience is organised by the student   T   F   N

18. Work experience is part-time work   T   F   N

19. Barbara has almost completed her course   T   F   N

20. Work experience is paid   T   F   N

21. The student has to write a report about the company   T   F   N

22. The company has to write a report about the student   T   F   N

23. Barbara has applied to other companies   T   F   N

24. *Circle the correct letter.*

     A   Barbara felt confident that she would be accepted by the company

     B   The secretary assured Barbara she would be accepted by the company

     C   Barbara hoped she would be accepted by the company

     D   Barbara did not feel confident she would be accepted by the company

Complete the message below.

MESSAGE

25. Name: _____

26. Miss   Ms   Mrs   Mr   *(Circle one)*

27. Address: No. _____

     Street: _____

     Suburb: *Forestville*

28. Postcode: _____

29. Phone: _____

30. Best time to call: _____

NOTES

SECTION 4

Questions 31–40

31. *Circle the correct letter.*

    Which is the most dangerous seat in a car?

A	front left	**B**	front right
C	back left	**D**	back right

32. *Circle **TWO** letters.*

    From the following list, which **TWO** things have the greatest effect on the severity of injury in a car accident?

    A   age of driver

    B   blood alcohol level

    C   sex of driver

    D   seating position

    E   kind of vehicle

    F   age of vehicle

Questions 33–34

    What **TWO** factors have previously been the focus of safe driver education?

33.   _____

34.   _____

35. *Write **TWO** words.*

    Which kind of vehicle is the most dangerous?

    _____

Complete the table below with information from the talk.

	Speed of car (kph)	Percentage chance of injury requiring treatment at		Percentage chance of death
		1) scene of accident	2) hospital	
Passenger	42	10–20	60–70	36. _____
Driver	37. _____	70	30	38. _____
	39. _____	60	40	0

40. *Circle **TWO** letters.*

Which **TWO** reasons are suggested to explain why passengers are more at risk than drivers, in an accident?

A   drivers automatically turn to the right

B   drivers usually protect themselves

C   cars tend to turn to the right when the driver brakes

D   cars are not designed very well

LISTENING TEST 2

SECTION 1

Questions 1–12

Circle the correct letter.

Example:
Alex has recently...
A started at university   Ⓒ completed university
B begun a new job   D finished work

---

1. *Write your answer in the space provided.*

   How long is the train trip to the city? _____

2. *Circle the correct letter.*

   What time does Alex's train leave the city?

10:30	22:30	10:13	20:30
A	**B**	**C**	**D**

3. *Write your answer in the space provided.*

   Where can the public see the submarine? _____

4. *Circle the correct letter.*

   Which is Alex's current car?

   A

   B

   C

   D

Questions 5–6

Name two kinds of movies John would enjoy very much.

5. _____

6. _____

Questions 7–12

Complete the form below.

Panorama Camera Store

Repair Form

7. Customer name: *Alex* _____

8. Address: _____

    _____ *Howell*

9. Post code: _____

10. Telephone number: _____

11. Date ready for collection: _____

12. Date customer will collect: _____

SECTION 2

Questions 13–20

*As you listen, fill the gaps above the numbers. The first one, **Wine Science**, has been done as an example.*

Title	Author	Edition	Cost	Condition
__Wine__ __Science__ *Example*	Bookman	_____ _____ 13.	_____ _____ 14.	Fair
_____ _____ 15.	Maclean	1993	_____ _____ 16.	Quite Good
Wine Making	Brown	_____ _____ 17.	_____ _____ 18.	Immaculate
Red Wines of the world	Able	_____ _____ 19.	$25	_____ _____ 20.

26

SECTION 3

Questions 21–31

21. *Circle the correct letter.*

    What is Terry's job?

    A   Environment Reports Officer

    B   Environment and Resources Officer

    C   Office worker

    D   University Resources Officer

22. *Name* **TWO** *sources of office paper waste.*

    _____   _____

23. *Name* **TWO** *of the paper products that are produced from recycled office paper.*

    _____   _____

24. *Circle the correct letter.*

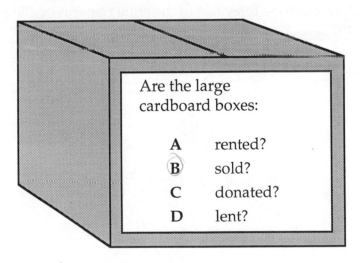

Are the large cardboard boxes:

    A   rented?
    B   sold?
    C   donated?
    D   lent?

27

Fill in the table below.

Paper categories	Definitions
25. _____ paper	paper used on one side only
26. _____ paper	paper used on both sides
scrap paper	paper that is 27. _____ or is in 28. _____ and is otherwise not useful
29. _____ paper	includes buff-coloured envelopes and 30. _____

31. Which **ONE** word does Terry use to describe paper recycling as increasing in popularity?

_____

SECTION 4

Questions 32–40

Questions 32–34

Circle the correct letter.

32. Technology is often described as:

    A   development of innovation   **B**   generation of research

    C   transformation of knowledge   **D**   application of scientific ideas

33. Which part of the diagram below is compared to science?

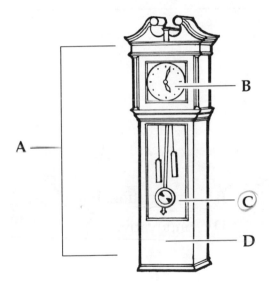

34. Development is:

    A   processing an idea then controlling the product or service
    B   researching a product or service then developing an idea
    C   producing a product or service then selling it
    D   generating an idea then turning it into a product or service

Questions 35–38

*Answer questions 35–38 using **NO MORE THAN TWO** words for each answer or each part of an answer.*

35. Why is it that companies do not develop more new products?

    _____

36. Why is investment in record players not recommended?

    _____

37. Where can large research and development units still be found?

    _____

38. Name **TWO** places where commercialisation assistance can be obtained.

    _____   _____

Questions 39–40

Circle the correct letter

39. The commercialisation movement is:

    A   very popular   **B**   international

    C   national   **D**   innovative

40. Is the speaker optimistic about the future of the commercialisation of science and technology?

    A   yes   **B**   no

    C   perhaps   **D**   does not say

30

LISTENING TEST 3

SECTION 1

Questions 1–12

Questions 1–4

Circle the correct letter.

> *Example:*
>   The canteen closes at:
>
>   **A**   3.45   **(B)**   4.00
>
>   **C**   4.30   **D**   5.00

1.   The busiest time is:

     A   10.30   **B**   11.30

     C   12.30   **D**   3.00

2.   The most popular dessert is the:

A   chocolate cream cake

B   strawberry tart

C   apple pie

D   cream cake

3. Staff like:

A sandwiches

B croissants

C rolls

D hot meal on a plate

4. What do students do with their dirty dishes?

A

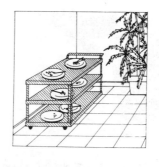

B

C

D

Questions 5–12

As you listen, fill in the details on the report with the information you hear.

POLICE REPORT

5. Surname _____

6. Address _____ *Rose Street,*

7. Suburb _____

8. Passport no. _____

9. Time lost *Between* _____ *and* _____

10. Bus no. _____

11. Where else reported? _____

12. What else missing? _____

_____

SECTION 2

Questions 13–22

Below is a summary of Adam and Sue's conversation. Complete the summary by writing ONE suitable word in the numbered spaces.

As a solicitor, Sue advises people about their 13. _____ in many different topic areas. One of the most interesting areas for overseas students is 14. _____ laws. People are often surprised to find that you are not allowed to bring 15. _____ into Australia because in many countries customs regulations pay little attention to this matter. They attach more importance to 16. _____ and 17. _____ . However, in Australia, you can't even take 18. _____ from one state to another. It doesn't matter whether you are travelling by 19. _____ or by 20. _____ . There are 21. _____ to remind you not to bring in any fruit. This is because of the need to protect 22. _____ against pests.

SECTION 3

Questions 23–29

*Answer each of the following questions with **NOT MORE THAN TWO** words.*

23. What was the Vietnamese student bringing in?

_____

24. What must every passenger coming into Australia sign?

_____

25. Did the student admit that he was carrying food in his luggage?

_____

26. What made it difficult for him to understand the officer's questions?

_____

27. Did he get his visa at the time he needed it?

_____

28. Who might have done his packing for him?

_____

29. What did his mother probably want to do?

_____

SECTION 4

Questions 30–38

Complete the advice below by writing **NO MORE THAN THREE** *words in the spaces provided.*

30. When you go out, remember _____ .

31. Don't keep _____ at home.

32. Don't let other people see you with _____ .

33. Carry your _____ with you at all times when away from home.

34. Never leave your car or bicycle _____ .

35. When you go out at night keep to _____ .

36. Only go out with people _____ .

37. While you are settling in, it is better to go out _____ .

38. Never get into _____ .

Reflections on the Listening Test

After you have finished each Listening test, check your answers in the Answer Key on page 177, then work through these reflection tasks. Thinking about each test and recalling how you felt before, during and after it, might help you when you eventually take the IELTS test.

1. Were you pleased with your performance?
    ❑ yes   ❑ no

2. How did you feel about the listening test? Was it
    ❑ easy   ❑ not too bad   ❑ difficult?

3. How much of what each speaker was saying could you follow?
    ❑ all of it   ❑ most of it   ❑ very little

4. How well could you understand the vocabulary in each test
    ❑ easily   ❑ reasonably well   ❑ with difficulty?

5. If you got less than a perfect score, identify the sections of the test where you had problems. Locate each section in the transcript and think about why you had problems. Was it to do with:
    a   rate of speech?
    b   unknown vocabulary?
    c   unfamiliar accent?
    d   not understanding the question?
    e   nervousness?
    f   other?

    rate of speech: If one, or more than one of the speakers spoke too fast for you, listen to that part of the recording again. First, concentrate only on that section and see if you can follow the speaker. Listen once, without reading from the transcript. Then, check the transcript.

    unknown vocabulary: If there were words you didn't know, find any unknown vocabulary in the transcript and then look up these words in a dictionary, or ask someone.

    nervousness: Many people suffer from 'test nerves' but those who do well in tests are people who control their nerves rather than letting their nerves control them. We all know about and probably even have our own methods for coping with anxiety. If you became nervous during the practice tests, try to understand why. When you feel you can identify some reasons, make a list of some of the ways you might reduce the stress of taking a test. Think about how you can control your anxiety, when you eventually sit for the IELTS test.

READING PRACTICE TESTS

There are 9 reading practice tests

Time allowed for each test: 60 minutes

<u>Before you start</u>
Photocopy a reading test answer sheet on the next page.
Write your answers on the answer sheet.
When you have finished each test, check your answers with the answer key on pages 178–181.

READING ANSWER SHEET

Photocopy this page to write your answers to each Reading test you practise.

Module taken:

Academic ▭
General Training ▭

Test number:

Enter the number in the boxes and shade the number in the grid.

00	10	20	30	40	50	60	70	80	90
▭	▭	▭	▭	▭	▭	▭	▭	▭	▭

↑ ▭▭ ↓

0	1	2	3	4	5	6	7	8	9
▭	▭	▭	▭	▭	▭	▭	▭	▭	▭

#	Answer
1	NO
2	Yes
3	
4	
5	
6	
7	
8	
9	
10	
11	
12	C
13	B
14	B
15	
16	
17	
18	X
19	X
20	
21	
22	
23	
24	
25	

#	Answer
26	
27	A
28	
29	NO
30	NO
31	NG
32	
33	
34	
35	
36	
37	
38	
39	
40	
41	
42	
43	
44	

Band Score		Reading Total	

READING TEST 1

QUESTIONS 1–14

*You are advised to spend about 15 minutes on **Questions 1–14** which refer to Reading Passage 1 below.*

READING PASSAGE 1

FINDING THE LOST FREEDOM

1. The private car is assumed to have widened our horizons and increased our mobility. When we consider our children's mobility, they can be driven to more places (and more distant places) than they could visit without access to a motor vehicle. However, allowing our cities to be dominated by cars has progressively eroded children's independent mobility. Children have lost much of their freedom to explore their own neighbourhood or city without adult supervision. In recent surveys, when parents in some cities were asked about their own childhood experiences, the majority remembered having more, or far more, opportunities for going out on their own, compared with their own children today. They had more freedom to explore their own environment.

2. Children's independent access to their local streets may be important for their own personal, mental and psychological development. Allowing them to get to know their own neighbourhood and community gives them a 'sense of place'. This depends on 'active exploration', which is not provided for when children are passengers in cars. (Such children may see more, but they learn less.) Not only is it important that children be able to get to local play areas by themselves, but walking and cycling journeys to school and to other destinations provide genuine play activities in themselves.

3. There are very significant time and money costs for parents associated with transporting their children to school, sport and to other locations. Research in the United Kingdom estimated that this cost, in 1990, was between 10 billion and 20 billion pounds.

4. The reduction in children's freedom may also contribute to a weakening of the sense of local community. As fewer children and adults use the streets as pedestrians, these streets become less sociable places. There is less opportunity for children and adults to have the spontaneous exchanges that help to engender a feeling of community. This in itself may exacerbate fears associated with assault and molestation of children, because there are fewer adults available who know their neighbours' children, and who can look out for their safety.

5. The extra traffic involved in transporting children results in increased traffic congestion, pollution and accident risk. As our roads become more dangerous, more parents drive their children to more places, thus contributing to increased levels of danger for the remaining pedestrians. Anyone who has experienced either the reduced volume of traffic in peak hour during school holidays, or the traffic jams near schools at the end of a school day, will not need convincing about these points. Thus, there are also important environmental implications of children's loss of freedom.

6. As individuals, parents strive to provide the best upbringing they can for their children. However, in doing so, (e.g. by driving their children to sport, school or recreation) parents may be contributing to a more dangerous environment for children generally. The idea that 'streets are for cars and back yards and playgrounds are for children' is a strongly held belief, and parents have little choice as individuals but to keep their children off the streets if they want to protect their safety.

7. In many parts of Dutch cities, and some traffic calmed precincts in Germany, residential streets are now places where cars must give way to pedestrians. In these areas, residents are accepting the view that the function of streets

is not solely to provide mobility for cars. Streets may also be for social interaction, walking, cycling and playing. One of the most important aspects of these European cities, in terms of giving cities back to children, has been a range of 'traffic calming' initiatives, aimed at reducing the volume and speed of traffic. These initiatives have had complex interactive effects, leading to a sense that children have been able to 'recapture' their local neighbourhood, and more importantly, that they have been able to do this in safety. Recent research has demonstrated that children in many German cities have significantly higher levels of freedom to travel to places in their own neighbourhood or city than children in other cities in the world.

8. Modifying cities in order to enhance children's freedom will not only benefit children. Such cities will become more environmentally sustainable, as well as more sociable and more livable for all city residents. Perhaps it will be our concern for our children's welfare that convinces us that we need to challenge the dominance of the car in our cities.

Questions 1–5

Read statements 1–5 which relate to Paragraphs **1, 2,** and **3** of the reading passage. Answer **T** if the statement is true, **F** if the statement is false, or **NI** if there is no information given in the passage. Write your answers in the spaces numbered 1–5 on the answer sheet. One has been done for you as an example.

Example:	The private car has made people more mobile.
Answer:	**T**

1.   The private car has <u>helped</u> children have <u>more opportunities</u> to learn.

2.   Children are more <u>independent</u> today than they used to be.

3.   <u>Walking</u> and <u>cycling</u> to school allows children to learn more.

4.   Children usually <u>walk</u> or <u>cycle</u> to school.

5.   Parents save time and money by driving children to school.

Questions 6–9

In Paragraphs **4** and **5**, there are **FOUR** problems stated. These problems, numbered as questions 6–9, are listed below. Each of these problems has a cause, listed **A–G**. Find the correct cause for each of the problems and write the corresponding letter **A–G**, in the spaces numbered 6–9 on the answer sheet. One has been done for you as an example.
There are more causes than problems so you will not use all of them and you may use any cause more than once.

Problems		Causes	

Example: low sense of community feeling	Answer F

6.	streets become less sociable	A	few adults know local children
7.	fewer chances for meeting friends	B	fewer people use the streets
8.	fears of danger for children	C	increased pollution
9.	higher accident risk	D	streets are less friendly
		E	less traffic in school holidays
		F	reduced freedom for children
		G	more children driven to school

Questions 10–14

Questions 10–14 are statement beginnings which represent information given in Paragraphs **6**, **7** and **8**. In the box below, there are some statement endings numbered **i–x**. Choose the correct ending for each statement. Write your answers **i–x**, in the spaces numbered 10–14 on the answer sheet. One has been done for you as an example.

There are more statement endings than you will need.

Example:	By driving their children to school, parents help create ...
Answer:	**i.**

10. Children should play ...

11. In some German towns, pedestrians have right of way ...

12. Streets should also be used for ...

13. Reducing the amount of traffic and the speed is ...

14. All people who live in the city will benefit if cities are ...

List of statement endings

i	... a dangerous environment.
ii	... modified.
iii	... on residential streets.
iv	... modifying cities.
v	... neighbourhoods.
vi	... socialising.
vii	... in backyards.
viii	... for cars.
ix	... traffic calming.
x	... residential.

READING PASSAGE 2

Rising seaS

Paragraph 1. INCREASED TEMPERATURES
The average air temperature at the surface of the earth has risen this century, as has the temperature of ocean surface waters. Because water expands as it heats, a warmer ocean means higher sea levels. We cannot say definitely that the temperature rises are due to the greenhouse effect; the heating may be part of a 'natural' variability over a long time-scale that we have not yet recognised in our short 100 years of recording. However, assuming the build up of greenhouse gases is responsible, and that the warming will continue, scientists—and inhabitants of low-lying coastal areas—would like to know the extent of future sea level rises.

Paragraph 2. ───────────────
Calculating this is not easy. Models used for the purpose have treated the ocean as passive, stationary and one-dimensional. Scientists have assumed that heat simply diffused into the sea from the atmosphere. Using basic physical laws, they then predict how much a known volume of water would expand for a given increase in temperature. But the oceans are not one-dimensional, and recent work by oceanographers, using a new model which takes into account a number of subtle facets of the sea— including vast and complex ocean currents—suggests that the rise in sea level may be less than some earlier estimates had predicted.

Paragraph 3. ───────────────
An international forum on climate change, in 1986, produced figures for likely sea-level rises of 20 cms and 1.4 m, corresponding to atmospheric temperature increases of 1.5° and 4.5° C respectively. Some scientists estimate that the ocean warming resulting from those temperature increases by the year 2050 would raise the sea level by between 10 cms and 40 cms. This model only takes into account the temperature effect on the oceans; it does not consider changes in sea level brought about by the melting of ice sheets and glaciers, and changes in groundwater storage. When we add on estimates of these, we arrive at figures for total sea-level rises of 15 cm and 70 cm respectively.

Paragraph 4. ───────────────
It's not easy trying to model accurately the enormous complexities of the ever-changing oceans, with their great volume, massive currents and sensitivity to the influence of land masses and the atmosphere. For example, consider how heat enters the ocean. Does it just 'diffuse' from the warmer air vertically into the water, and heat only the surface layer of the sea? (Warm water is less dense than cold, so it would not spread downwards.) Conventional models of sea-level rise have considered that this is the only method, but measurements have shown that the rate of heat transfer into the ocean by vertical diffusion is far lower in practice than the figures that many modellers have adopted.

Paragraph 5. ───────────────
Much of the early work, for simplicity, ignored the fact that water in the oceans moves in three dimensions. By movement, of course, scientists don't mean waves, which are too small individually to consider, but rather movement of vast volumes of water in huge currents. To understand the importance of this, we now need to consider another process—advection. Imagine smoke rising from a chimney. On a still day it will slowly spread out in all directions by means of diffusion. With a strong directional wind, however, it will all shift downwind. This process is advection—the transport of properties (notably heat and salinity in the ocean) by the movement of bodies of air or water, rather than by conduction or diffusion.

Paragraph **6.** ————————————————

Massive ocean currents called gyres do the moving. These currents have far more capacity to store heat than does the atmosphere. Indeed, just the top 3 m of the ocean contains more heat than the whole of the atmosphere. The origin of gyres lies in the fact that more heat from the Sun reaches the Equator than the Poles, and naturally heat tends to move from the former to the latter. Warm air rises at the Equator, and draws more air beneath it in the form of winds (the 'Trade Winds') that, together with other air movements, provide the main force driving the ocean currents.

Paragraph **7.** ————————————————

Water itself is heated at the Equator and moves poleward, twisted by the Earth's rotation and affected by the positions of the continents. The resultant broadly circular movements between about 10° and 40° North and South are clockwise in the Northern Hemisphere and anticlockwise in the Southern Hemisphere. They flow towards the east at mid latitudes in the equatorial region. They then flow towards the Poles, along the eastern sides of continents, as warm currents. When two different masses of water meet, one will move beneath the other, depending on their relative densities in the subduction process. The densities are determined by temperature and salinity. The convergence of water of different densities from the Equator and the Poles deep in the oceans causes continuous subduction. This means that water moves vertically as well as horizontally. Cold water from the Poles travels at depth—it is denser than warm water—until it emerges at the surface in another part of the world in the form of a cold current.

Paragraph **8.** HOW THE GREEN HOUSE EFFECT WILL CHANGE OCEAN TEMPERATURES

Ocean currents, in three dimensions, form a giant 'conveyor belt', distributing heat from the thin surface layer into the interior of the oceans and around the globe. Water may take decades to circulate in these 3–D gyres in the top kilometre of the ocean, and centuries in the deeper water. With the increased atmospheric temperatures due to the greenhouse effect, the oceans' conveyor belt will carry more heat into the interior. This subduction moves heat around far more effectively than simple diffusion. Because warm water expands more than cold when it is heated, scientists had presumed that the sea level would rise unevenly around the globe. It is now believed that these inequalities cannot persist, as winds will act to continuously spread out the water expansion. Of course, if global warming changes the strength and distribution of the winds, then this 'evening-out' process may not occur, and the sea level could rise more in some areas than others.

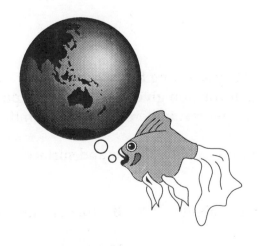

Questions 15–20

There are 8 paragraphs numbered **1–8** in Reading Passage 2. The first paragraph and the last paragraph have been given headings. From the list below numbered **A–I**, choose a suitable heading for the remaining 6 paragraphs. Write your answers **A–I**, in the spaces numbered 15–20 on the answer sheet.
There are more headings than paragraphs, so you will not use all the headings.

List of headings

A THE GYRE PRINCIPLE
B THE GREENHOUSE EFFECT
C HOW OCEAN WATERS MOVE
D STATISTICAL EVIDENCE
E THE ADVECTION PRINCIPLE
F DIFFUSION VERSUS ADVECTION
G FIGURING THE SEA LEVEL CHANGES
H ESTIMATED FIGURES
I THE DIFFUSION MODEL

15.   Paragraph **2**

16.   Paragraph **3**

17.   Paragraph **4**

18.   Paragraph **5**

19.   Paragraph **6**

20.   Paragraph **7**

Questions 21 and 22

Answer questions 21 and 22 by selecting the correct answer to complete each sentence according to the information given in the reading passage. Write your answers **A, B, C** or **D** in the spaces numbered 21 and 22 on the answer sheet.

21. Scientists do not know for sure why the air and surface of ocean temperatures are rising because:

A   there is too much variability

B   there is not enough variability

C   they have not been recording these temperatures for enough time

D   the changes have only been noticed for 100 years

22. New research leads scientists to believe that:

    A the oceans are less complex   ✓ **B** the oceans are more complex

    C the oceans will rise more than expected   **D** the oceans will rise less than expected

Question 23

Look at the following list of factors **A-F** and select **THREE** which are mentioned in the reading passage which may contribute to the rising ocean levels. Write the **THREE** corresponding letters **A–F**, in the space numbered 23 on the answer sheet.

List of factors

    A   thermal expansion

    B   melting ice

    C   increased air temperature

    D   higher rainfall

    E   changes in the water table

    F   increased ocean movement

Questions 24–28

Read each of the following statements, 24–28. According to the information in the reading passage, if the statement is true, write **T**, if it is false, write **F** and if there is no information about the statement in the reading passage, write **NI**. Write your answers in the spaces numbered 24–28 on the answer sheet.

24. The surface layer of the oceans is warmed by the atmosphere.

25. Advection of water changes heat and salt levels.

26. A gyre holds less heat than there is in the atmosphere.

27. The process of subduction depends on the water density.

28. The sea level is expected to rise evenly over the Earth's surface.

READING PASSAGE 3

NEW RULES FOR THE PAPER GAME

1. Computerised data storage and electronic mail were to have heralded the paperless office. But, contrary to expectations, paper consumption throughout the world shows no sign of abating. In fact, consumption, especially of printing and writing papers, continues to increase. World demand for paper and board is now expected to grow faster than the general economic growth in the next 15 years. Strong demand will be underpinned by the growing industrialization of South-East Asia, the re-emergence of paper packaging, greater use of facsimile machines and photocopiers, and the popularity of direct-mail advertising. It is possible that by 2007, world paper and board demand will reach 455 million tonnes, compared with 241 million tonnes in 1991.

2. The pulp and paper industry has not been badly affected by the electronic technologies that promised a paperless society. But what has radically altered the industry's structure is pressure from another front—a more environmentally conscious society driving an irreversible move towards cleaner industrial production. The environmental consequences of antiquated pulp mill practices and technologies had marked this industry as one in need of reform. Graphic descriptions of deformed fish and thinning populations, particularly in the Baltic Sea where old pulp mills had discharged untreated effluents for 100 years, have disturbed the international community.

3. Until the 1950s, it was common for pulp mills and other industries to discharge untreated effluent into rivers and seas. The environmental effects were at the time either not understood, or regarded as an acceptable cost of economic prosperity in an increasingly import-oriented world economy. But greater environmental awareness has spurred a fundamental change in attitude in the community, in government and in industry itself.

4. Since the early 1980s, most of the world-scale pulp mills in Scandinavia and North America have modernised their operations, outlaying substantial amounts to improve production methods. Changes in mill design and processes have been aimed at minimising the environmental effects of effluent discharge while at the same time producing pulp with the whiteness and strength demanded by the international market. The environmental impetus is taking this industry even further, with the focus now on developing processes that may even eliminate waste-water discharges. But the ghost of the old mills continues to haunt the industry today. In Europe, companies face a flood of environment-related legislation. In Germany, companies are now being held responsible for the waste they create.

5. Pulp is the porridge-like mass of plant fibres from which paper is made. Paper makers choose the type of plant fibre and the processing methods, depending on what the end product will be used for: whether it is a sturdy packing box, a smooth sheet of writing paper or a fragile tissue. In wood, which is the source of about 90% of the world's paper production, fibres are bound together by lignin, which gives the unbleached pulp a brown colour. The pulping stage separates the wood into fibres so they are suitable for paper making. Pulping can be done by mechanical grinding, or by chemical treatment in which woodchips are 'cooked' with chemicals, or by a combination of both methods.

6. Kraft pulping is the most widely used chemical process for producing pulp with the strength required by the high-quality paper market. It is now usually carried out in a continuous process in a large vessel called a digester. Woodchips are fed from a pile into the top of the digester. In the digester, the chips are cooked in a solution called white liquor,

composed of caustic soda (sodium hydroxide) and sodium sulphide. The chips are cooked at high temperatures of up to 170° C for up to three hours. The pulp is then washed and separated from the spent cooking liquor which has turned dark and is now appropriately called black liquor. An important feature of kraft pulping is a chemical recovery system which recycles about 95% of the cooking chemicals and produces more than enough energy to run the mill. In a series of steps involving a furnace and tanks, some of the black liquor is transformed into energy, while some is regenerated into the original white cooking liquor. The recovery system is an integral part of production in the pulp and paper industry. The pulp that comes out has little lignin left in the fibres. Bleaching removes the last remain-ing lignin and brightens the pulp. Most modern mills have modified their pulping processes to remove as much of the lignin as possible before the pulp moves to the bleaching stage.

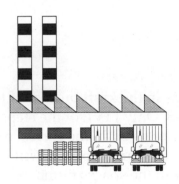

Questions 29–32

Below is a list of possible factors, **A–G,** which will influence the amount of paper being used in the future. From the list, choose **FOUR** factors which are mentioned in Paragraph **1** of the reading passage. Write your answers **A–G,** in the spaces numbered 29–32 on the answer sheet.

List of factors

    A   more people read newspapers

    B   increased use of paper bags

    C   increased book production for education

    D   wider use of sign post advertising

    E   increased use of fax machines

    F   wider use of leaflet advertising

    G   greater use of duplicating machines

The following **THREE** statements are summaries of Paragraphs **2**, **3** and **4** respectively. However, they are incomplete. Complete each of the statements using **NO MORE THAN THREE WORDS FROM THE TEXT**. Write your answers in the spaces numbered 33–35 on the answer sheet.

33.   The international community has begun to demand ...
34.   In the past, the environmental effects of pulp mill practices, were probably a price to pay for ...
35.   Some paper mills have recently modernised their mill design in order to decrease ...

Questions 36–40

Below is a list of possible steps in the kraft process of turning wood chips into paper. They are numbered **1–8.** Only **FIVE** of the steps listed below are mentioned in the passage. The steps are not listed in the correct order. Decide which steps are mentioned and write them **in the correct order**. Write the appropriate number for each step **in the correct order** in the spaces numbered 36–40 on the answer sheet.

1   the chips are cooked

2   the fibres are bound by lignin

3   the pulp is bleached

4   woodchips are put into a pile

5   the pulp is dried

6   the pulp is removed from the black liquor

7   the chips are put into the white liquor

8   the pulp is washed

READING TEST 2

QUESTIONS 1–14

You are advised to spend about 15 minutes on **Questions 1–14** *which refer to Reading Passage 1 below.*

READING PASSAGE 1

HOW TO RAISE A BRIGHT CHILD

Teachers and other specialists in early childhood education recognise that children develop at different rates. Given anything that resembles a well-rounded life—with adults and other children to listen to, talk to, to do things with—their minds will acquire naturally all the skills required for further learning.

Take, for example, reading. The two strongest predictors of whether children will learn to read easily and well at school are whether they have learned the names and the sounds of the letters of the alphabet before they start school. That may seem to imply that letter names and sounds should be deliberately taught to young children, because these skills will not happen 'naturally'.

But in all the research programs where they have done just that—instructed children, rehearsed the names and sounds over and over—the results are disappointing. The widely accepted explanation is that knowledge of the alphabet, for it to work in helping one to read, has to be deeply embedded in the child's mind. That comes from years of exposure and familiarity with letters, from being read to, from playing with magnetic letters, drawing and fiddling with computers.

So parents can do some things to help, although many do these things spontaneously. Instead of reading a story straight through, the reader should pause every so often and ask questions—but not questions which can be answered by a yes or no. Extend their answers, suggest alternative possibilities and pose progressively more challenging questions.

And with arithmetic, do not explicitly sit down and teach children about numbers, but all through those early years count when walking up steps. Recite nursery rhymes. Talk to children. Say this is a *red* apple, that is a *green* one. Please get *three* eggs out of the fridge for me.

The technical term in vogue for this subtle structuring of children's early learning is 'scaffolding'. Based on recent extensions of the work of the Russian psychologist Lev Vygotsky, the idea is that there are things a child may be almost ready to do. Anna, for example, cannot tie a shoelace by herself, but if an adult or a competent child forms one of the loops for her, she will soon learn to do the rest. Applying this concept to older children, one wonderful teacher has her children keep lists of 'Words I Can Almost Spell'.

While this has all the hallmarks of common sense, it represents a significant change of emphasis from the ideas of Piaget, which have dominated the theory of early childhood learning. The child in Piaget's theory looks, more than anything, like a little scientist—exploring the environment, observing, experimenting, thinking and slowly coming to his or her conclusions about how the world works. The image is of a rather solitary pursuit with all the real action in the child's head.

The Vygotsky model re-introduces all the people who also inhabit the child's world—parents, care-givers, relatives, siblings and all those other children at play or school. They are not simply noise, clattering in the background while the child's developing mind struggles on its own. The cognitive development of the child, that is, the learning of colours or numbers or letters—depends on learning how to interact socially, how to learn from the people (as well as the things) in the environment.

What is important is that the child develops the range of social skills—being able to express a

49

preference, knowing how to take turns, being able to stand up for themselves, being able to get into a group, being able to make decisions, being able to share, having confidence to go off on their own. These all require careful nurturing. No one is telling parents to not think about their children's development. It is just that it is more important to think about a child's desire to chat and the importance of social behaviour and play activity, than the actually more trivial markers of intellectual achievement such as being the first kid in the group to cut out a circle that looks like a circle.

Questions 1–3

Read each of the following statements. According to the information in the passage, if the statement is true write **T**, if the statement is false write **F**, and if there is no information about the statement in the passage, write **NI.** Write your answers in the spaces numbered 1–3 on the answer sheet. One has been done for you as an example.

> *Example:* It is generally accepted that children learn at different rates
> *Answer:* **T**

1. Sounds of letters have to be taught.

2. Children learn by asking questions.

3. Children should be taught to count before they start school.

Questions 4–8

Each of the following statements represents theories of childhood learning. Read each statement. If the statement represents the theory of Vygotsky, write **V**. If the statement represents the theory of Piaget, write **P**. If the statement does not represent the theory of either Piaget or Vygotsky, write **N**. Write the answers in the spaces numbered 4–8 on the answer sheet. One has been done for you as an example.

> *Example:* 'Scaffolding' is a term meaning subtle structuring.
> *Answer:* **V**

4. There is always something a child can just about do or learn.

5. Children learn by watching and doing.

6. Children learn when they have time alone to reflect.

7. Regular study habits are important for cognitive and moral development.

8. Play helps learning.

Questions 9–14

The following paragraph is the final paragraph of the reading passage. There are some words missing. Choose **ONE** word for each space from the list of words below. Write the correct word in the spaces numbered 9–14 on the answer sheet. One has been done for you as an example.

There are more words than spaces so you won't use all the words.

> What in fact, worries the ...*Example*... and professional care-givers far more...
> *Answer*:   teachers

... than any possible slowness in a child's developing a few 9. _Cognitive_ tasks is the pressure that some parents exert for their children to be made to learn too quickly. It has to be admitted that 10. _pushing_ often appears to work. It is possible to speed up their acquisition of academic 11. _skills_ , to give them an edge, as it were. But there is a price—because there is a paradox. Though it looks as if the children are 12. _achieving_ , more often than not they are losing the one ingredient that will determine 13. _success_ in the longer term. Their self-direction, self-motivation, is being taken away from them. By being told what to do, by being told what is really important, by being channelled, they do not develop the essential ability of finding 14. _goals_ for themselves.

List of words

success	teachers	cognitive
ability	goals	achievement
successful	intelligent	skills
pushing	achieving	academic

*You are advised to spend about 20 minutes on **Questions 15–27** which refer to Reading Passage 2 below.*

READING PASSAGE 2

THE VALUE OF DRIVER TRAINING

1. Most fatal accidents involve a disproportionately high number of men under the age of 25. A report on young driver research prepared last year by Monash University's accident research centre found that in 1990 and 1991, almost a third of the people killed in road crashes were drivers under 25, yet this age group represents only 14 per cent of the population. The report, which also updated a review of international literature about, among other things, driver training, also reached what many would consider a startling conclusion: training and education where they occur—principally in the US—do not appear to reduce younger drivers' risk of crashing.

2. The Monash University researchers looked at crash information from New South Wales for 1986 to 1990, from Victoria for 1984 to 1990 and from South Australia for 1986 to 1990. The only Australian evidence which possibly indicates that counter-measures targeted specifically at young/novice drivers have been effective comes from evaluations of zero blood alcohol concentration legislation. (In 1989, all Australian governments agreed from 1991 on, to ban provisional drivers from drink-driving at any level, and to extend the provisional licence to three years).

3. The Monash researchers also looked at United States road-crash information for 1989 on 6.6 million police-reported crashes involving fatalities, injuries and motor vehicle damage. The researchers looked at a sample of 44,000 crashes. The conclusion was that the available literature gives a pessimistic view of the efficacy of driver training and education, reflected in the inability to produce drivers safer than those who have not been trained. One study on driver training in the US was conducted in DeKalb county, Georgia between 1977 and 1981. 16,000 school students were split into three groups: one group received 70 hours practical driver education training, another a brief, school based course and the third no school-based driver education. Those comprehensively trained were 16 per cent more likely to get their licences, but 11 per cent more likely to crash and eight per cent more likely to get traffic fines.

4. In 1985, the researchers who conducted that study then reviewed 14 studies of defensive-driver training courses and concluded that though people who attended such courses received fewer traffic fines, they did not have fewer crashes. Despite the intuitive conclusion that safe driving should be teachable (like many practical skills), there is insufficient evidence about the ability of practical driver-training to reduce crashes for the general driving population.

5. The Monash University report into young drivers concluded that younger drivers were more likely to take risks at night, younger men were more likely to take risks than younger women, but younger women appeared to have 'greater skills deficiency'. Overall, the researchers concluded that it appears that vehicle-control skills improve rapidly with increasing experience but that their development is still incomplete after one or two years and possibly after considerably longer periods.

The paragraphs in the reading passage are numbered **1–5**. Below is a list of paragraph headings labelled **A–I**. For each question 15–18, select the most suitable paragraph heading from the list and write your answers **A–I**, in the spaces numbered 15–18 on the answer sheet. The first one has been done for you as an example.

There are more headings than you will need, so you won't use them all.

Example:	Paragraph **1**
Answer:	**G**

15. Paragraph **2**

16. Paragraph **3**

17. Paragraph **4**

18. Paragraph **5**

List of headings

A	Looking at young drivers
B	Do driving courses prevent accidents?
C	Results of safety campaigns
D	A United States study
E	Defensive driving—fewer traffic fines
F	Male and female drivers
G	The Monash University report
H	An international review
I	The situation in the United States

Read each of the following statements numbered 19–23. If the statement is true, write **T,** if the statement is not true, write **F**, and if there is no information about the statement in the passage, write **NI**. Write your answers in the spaces numbered 19–23 on the answer sheet. One has been done for you as an example.

Example:	Approximately one third of people killed in road accidents are under 25 years old.
Answer:	**T**

19. More men than women are killed in road crashes.

20. The laws against drink-driving have helped prevent road accidents.

21. Young drivers who are taught to drive at school have fewer accidents.

22. Driver training for young drivers is compulsory in the United States.

23. All young people who undergo driver training get a driving licence.

Questions 24–27

Questions 24–27 are based on information from Paragraphs **4** and **5** of the reading passage. The statements are incomplete. Choose the correct ending for each statement from the list of statement endings **A–G**, in the box below. Write your answers **A–G**, in the spaces numbered 24–27 on the answer sheet. One has been done for you as an example.
There are more endings than you will need, so you won't use them all.

Example:	The researchers ...
Answer:	**H.**

24. Most people would expect that safe driving ...

25. People who do driver training courses ...

26. Young female drivers ...

27. Young male drivers ...

List of statement endings

A ... drive more at night.	**E** ... have few traffic fines.
B ... drive more carefully.	**F** ... have better driving skills.
C ... can not be taught.	**G** ... can be taught.
D ... have more traffic accidents.	**H** ... reviewed 14 studies.

*You are advised to spend about 25 minutes on **Questions 28–43** which refer to Reading Passage 3 below.*

READING PASSAGE 3

Human-powered Pumps for African Farmers

The plight of many African farmers and families in their search for water is well publicised in terms of disaster relief. Yet in many areas there are small dispersed sources of shallow ground water, which constitute a considerable resource. This is often not acknowledged by government agencies which think only in terms of large dams and perennial rivers.

African farmers are both ingenious and knowledgeable, and the work described here builds on these indigenous skills. The provision of effective and affordable human powered pumps transforms the possibilities of water supply for both small scale irrigation and domestic use. The field work was carried out predominantly in Zimbabwe, although more recently the pumps described here have been introduced in Kenya.

The need for water

An adequate supply of domestic water is vital for human health and hygiene. Despite the great progress made in the recent decade, the achievement of the goal of clean water for all is still a long way off. An adequate water supply is also vital for the production of food. In many parts of Africa, rainfall is a very unreliable provider of such water. For example, in Zimbabwe, Mupawose (1984) states that unreliable rainfall and the incidence of mid-season drought represent the single most critical uncertainty facing the Zimbabwean farmer today.

While staple foods such as maize and rice produced during the rainy season can be stored for consumption in the dry season, the same is not true of vegetables and fruit which are essential for good nutrition. Since the early part of this century, the answer to the problem of inadequate rainfall has been through the provision of conventional irrigation schemes.

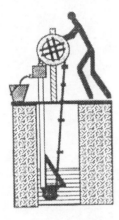

i. Traditional arrangement for vertical wells.

The failure of such schemes in many parts of Africa is well documented (Morris and Thom, 1990) and there is little hope of significant expansion in this sector.

Most of these irrigation schemes depend on the utilization of surface water resources, principally through the construction of dams. There is grave concern over the use of such dams because of their adverse impact on health, their displacement of successful farmers and the severe limitations on their useful life due to siltation (Wright, 1986; Arlosoroff *et al*. 1984; Bell *et al*, 1987).

In order to develop groundwater resources a suitable water lifting technology must be employed. While much work has been done on the development of power sources for water pumping (Hofkes and Visscher, 1986), for many people in rural Africa the use of human energy remains the only practical option (Lambert and Faulkner, 1991). In recent years there have been significant improvements in the design of handpumps for community use. However, community water points still suffer breakdowns and attempts to remedy this, through community managed pump maintenance schemes, are still far from universally successful.

The problems of community management could be avoided through the promotion of household supplies, where these are feasible.

An example of such a strategy in Zimbabwe is the program of upgrading family wells (Mtero and Chimbunde, 1991). However, most of the pumps developed for community use are either not available to individual households or are too expensive.

In recognition of the need for simple water-lifting technology, research was carried out to identify suitable water-lifting devices. Almost all existing human powered pumps tested could not supply water at more than about 0.3 litres per second, which is not sufficient for irrigation. Two designs were finally selected as the most promising for further development, the rope-washer and the treadle (Lambert and Faulkner, 1991).

ii. Modification for unlined ponds or streams.

Questions 28–30

Read the following statements. According to the information in the reading passage, if the statement is true, write **T**, if the statement is false, write **F**, and if there is no information about the statement in the reading passage, write **NI**. Write your answers in the spaces numbered 28–30 on the answer sheet. One has been done for you as an example.

| *Example*: | The difficulty in finding water in Africa is highly publicised. |
| *Answer*: | **T** |

28. Government agencies only consider dams and rivers as sources of water.

29. The pumps will help African villagers develop small industrial projects.

30. Most of the experimental work has been done in Zimbabwe and Kenya.

56

In the section after the subheading, **The need for water,** there are 7 references cited. Questions 31–36 list 6 of the references. Below is a list of statements **A–K** which are supported by the references. Match each reference (Questions 31–36) with its corresponding statement. Write the answers **A–K**, in the spaces numbered 31–36 on the answer sheet. One has been done for you as an example.

There are more statements than references so you won't use them all.

Example :	Lambert and Faulkner, 1991
Answer:	**K**

31. Mupawose, 1984

32. Morris and Thom, 1990

33. Wright, 1986; Arlosoroff et al, 1984; Bell et al, 1987

34. Hofkes and Visscher, 1986

35. Lambert and Faulkner, 1991

36. Mtero and Chimbunde, 1991

List of statements

A	Dams usually take up a lot of land so that farmers have to move somewhere else.
B	There has been little success with irrigation projects.
C	It is important to have an adequate water supply.
D	Human power is still cheaper and more readily available.
E	Rainfall is too little and too irregular when most needed.
F	Building dams has helped improve health.
G	There is a plan to improve individual domestic wells.
H	Experiments have been done to provide energy to pump water.
I	Most families cannot afford to buy pumps.
J	The design of hand pumps has improved lately.
K	The rope washer and treadle will help solve the problem.

Below is a paragraph explaining the design and development of the water pump. There are some words missing from the paragraph. From the list of words below, select **ONE** correct word for each space. Write your answer in the spaces numbered 37–43 on the answer sheet.

Pump design and development

The principle of the rope-washer pump is very old, dating back to ancient Rome and China. A pipe extends from the surface down to below the water 37. _level_. A loop of rope with washers attached is pulled by a 38. _pulley_ up through the pipe, and returns down to the water outside the pipe. Attached to the rope at intervals are washers whose 39. _diameter_ is slightly less than that of the pipe. As the rope and washers travel up 40. _inside_ the pipe, they draw water with them which discharges at the top of the pipe. Historically the pulley was fashioned from wood or steel with teeth to 41. _grip_ the washers on the rope. Considerable 42. _skill_ was needed to make a pulley capable of pulling a wet and slippery rope which was under tension from the 43. _weight_ of water in the pipe.

List of words

grip	height	level
length	inside	diameter
skill	weight	tension
centre	pulley	handle
size	depth	over
strength	middle	pump

READING TEST 3

QUESTIONS 1–17

*You are advised to spend about 20 minutes on **Questions 1–17** which refer to Reading Passage 1 below.*

READING PASSAGE 1

> # Traditional Vietnamese Medical Theory

1. The beliefs of Vietnamese folk medicine associate illness with the absence of any of the three souls which maintain life, intelligence, and the senses, or of the nine spirits which collectively sustain the living body. A number of rituals performed at childbirth, which are aimed at protecting the mother and the infant from medical and magical dangers, derive from these beliefs, but they play a relatively limited role in medical behaviour generally. Conversely, Chinese medicine plays a major role in the maintenance and restoration of health and is observed by ethnic Vietnamese and by Vietnamese-Chinese. Principles from Chinese medicine provide the scripting for the management of birth for both groups, and more generally, establish guidelines whereby good health may be maintained.

2. According to Sino-Vietnamese medical theory, the body has two vital and opposite life forces which capture the essence of *yin* (breath) and *yang* (blood) in accordance with the 'five evolutive phases' (wood, fire, earth, metal and water). The proper circulation and balance of the *yin* and *yang* ensure the healthy circulation of blood and thus good health; disequilibrium and disharmony cause ill health. Illness, physical and mental, can be identified by the imbalance or excess of *yin* over *yang* or *yang* over *yin*. Foods and medicine, also classified according to their reputed intrinsic nature as *yin* (cold) and *yang* (hot), may be taken therapeutically to correct the imbalance resulting from ill health, or to correct imbalance due to the overindulgence in a food manifestly excessively 'hot' or 'cold', or due to age or changed physiological status (for example, pregnancy).

3. Foodstuffs may also be identified as tonic or antitonic, toxic or poison, or as having wind. A further small group of foods are ascribed magical properties. Other foods may be classified as neutral or remain outside any classification system, and hence have no overt therapeutic use.

4. While the classification of foods as hot, cold, tonic, poison, windy, magic and neutral is based on the intrinsic nature of the foods, in practice they are identified predominantly according to their physical effects on the body. Ultimately, the system is both individual and arbitrary, and there appears no firm correlation to the raw and cooked states of the food, the method of cooking, the spiciness, or the calorific value of the food.

5. In general, leafy vegetables, and most fruit are classified as cold and are said to cool the body; meat, condiments, alcohol, and fatty foods are classified as hot and are said to heat the body. Tonic foods, believed to increase the volume of blood and to promote health and energy, include 'protein-rich' foods, high fat, sugar, and carbohydrate foods (fried food, sweet fruit, honey and rice), and medicines (alcohol and vitamins). Sour foods, and sometimes raw and cold foods, tend to be considered antitonic and are believed to deplete the volume of blood. Wind foods include raw foods, leafy vegetables, and fruit, and often are classified as cold; they reputedly cause wind illness such as rheumatism and arthritis. Beef, mutton, fowl, fish, glutinous rice, and long bananas are considered potentially toxic and may cause convulsions, skin irritation and infection.

There are 5 paragraphs in Reading Passage 1 Traditional Vietnamese Medical Theory. Below is a list of possible headings for the paragraphs. The headings are numbered **A–H**. From the list, choose the best heading for each paragraph. Write your answer **A–H**, in the spaces numbered 1–4 on the answer sheet. One has been done for you as an example.

There are more headings than paragraphs, so you won't use all of them.

Example:	Paragraph **3**
Answer:	**B**

List of headings

A	Rituals for childbirth
B	Simple classification of foods
C	Blood and breath
D	Detailed classification of foods
E	The development of Vietnamese medical theory
F	Cooling and heating foods
G	Theory and practice in food classification
H	The components of the body life forces

1. Paragraph **1**

2. Paragraph **2**

3. Paragraph **4**

4. Paragraph **5**

Answer questions 5–9 using **NO MORE THAN TWO WORDS TAKEN FROM THE TEXT**. Write your answers in the spaces numbered 5–9 on the answer sheet.

5. What are the life forces of the body?

6. What **TWO** kinds of illness can be caused by a lack of balance between the life forces?

7. Name **TWO** life changes which may cause an imbalance of life forces in the body.

8. What criterion decides the theoretical classification of foods?

9. What criterion decides the actual classification of foods?

Questions 10–17

Below is a table representing the classification of foods into the therapeutic types according to traditional Vietnamese medical theory. There are some gaps in the information. Complete the table using information from the reading passage. Write **NO MORE THAN THREE WORDS FOR EACH ANSWER**. Write your answers in the spaces numbered 10–17 on the answer sheet.

Table of food classification

CLASS	FOOD	EFFECT
cold	leafy vegetables, some fruit	cooling
hot	meat, alcohol, fatty foods	heating
10. _____	honey, rice	11. _____
12. _____	13. _____	deplete blood volume
wind	raw foods, fruit	14. _____
15. _____	beef, fowl	16. _____
17. _____	(not described)	(not described)

You are advised to spend about 20 minutes on **Questions 18–28** which refer to Reading Passage 2 below.

READING PASSAGE 2

The New Supersonic Boom

As the world's only supersonic passenger jet approaches its 26th birthday, a worldwide race is underway to build the Concorde II. The British Airways fleet of seven has as little as 10 years' flying time left. British Airways has challenged designers to come up with its successor before the fleets, operated by BA and Air France for nearly 20 years, have exhausted their commercial lives. British Aerospace is working with French and German partners to develop a successor capable of carrying three times as many passengers. Racing against them are the Americans, also working toward a supersonic passenger plane for the 21st century.

The projected development cost is a minimum $10 billion—so high that only one version is likely to be built in the foreseeable future. BAe and Aerospatiale, which pioneered Concorde I, have been joined by Daimler Benz Aerospace on the joint Concorde II research project. The European Supersonic Research Program (ESRP) will be funded by all three countries. They also are involved in wider-ranging talks with Italian, Japanese and Russian organizations under the umbrella of the International Supersonic Study Group. Japanese Aircraft Industries, the Alenia Company of Italy and the Tupolev Design Bureau have been looking at environmental requirements, certification bases, market potential, global co-operation and business compatibility.

British Aerospace is looking for a plane holding a minimum of 200 passengers, compared to Concorde I's 100. The aircraft would have to be capable of flying between 5500 and 6500 miles at a cruising speed of Mach 2.5. The British Aerospace idea is for a 90m-long aircraft carrying 289 passengers instead of 60m-long Concorde I's 4000 miles at Mach 2. Long distance air travel is constantly increasing and passengers are asking for more

direct flights with increased comfort. Supersonic flights must not cost significantly more than normal flights and that must be one of the primary objectives. The market for a new commercial supersonic aircraft could be between 500 and 1000.

In the United States, Boeing and McDonnell Douglas are working on a successor plane with the aid of a $1.5 billion grant from the National Aeronautics and Space Administration (NASA). The first phase of the project began in the US in 1989, with NASA's High Speed Research Program (HSR I), which focused solely on environmental issues, such as noise and pollution, associated with supersonic travel. The second phase, HSR II, will move toward the construction of an aerodynamic craft capable of withstanding the rigours of daily supersonic travel.

Boeing and McDonnell Douglas have demonstrated that supersonic travel could be economically feasible and that demand exists for time-saving travel. Developments are expected to more than halve the time it now takes to fly between London and New York, and between Los Angeles and Tokyo. Even though it is accepted supersonic jets will be banned from flying over populated areas, there are still 150 routes of more than 3000km between 81 major cities which they could use. Rolls Royce is working on a suitable Variable Cycle Engine which will be quieter and faster than anything now available. It is hoped it will be acceptable for some overland flights, such as Siberia and northern Canada. It will have to be capable of cruising comfortably and economically at subsonic speeds using a turbofan, before the turbojet takes the craft up to supersonic speeds over the seas. It is believed that Concorde II is feasible and that technically it could be produced today. The Boeing group is looking at 300-seat 5000-mile (8000km) range, Mach 2.4 aircraft which could make extensive use of composite materials. It probably will take the full co-operation of Europe, the US and Japan to achieve.

It appears that there are also plans to build Concorde III, an exclusive supersonic jet to carry 12 passengers—a British Aerospace blueprint designed for world leaders and the wealthy. And there is a joint American-Russian venture for a similar aircraft, involving Gulfstream Aerospace Sukhoi Design Bureau. While many share this dream, it is not expected that such aircraft will enter service before the year 2010.

Questions 18–23.

Below is a table with comparative information about Concorde I, the European version of Concorde II and the American version of Concorde II. There is some information missing from the table. Complete the table using information from the reading passage. Write your answers in the spaces numbered 18–23 on the answer sheet. One has been done for you as an example.

| | CONCORDE I | CONCORDE II | |
		European version	American version
capacity	*Example:* 100	18. _____	*300*
distance	*4000 miles*	19. _____	20. _____
speed	21. _____	*2.5 Mach*	22. _____
length	*60m*	23. _____	*(not given)*

63

Look at the following statements **A-H**. According to Reading Passage 2, which **FOUR** statements are **TRUE**. Choose from the appropriate letters, **A-H**, and write them in the spaces numbered 24–27 on the answer sheet. The answers may be written in any order.

List of statements

A	Concorde II will be ready for commercial use in 10 years.
B	Daily use of supersonic aircraft causes structural problems.
C	The new supersonic jet should be twice as fast as the current one.
D	Only wealthy people will be able to travel on the new planes.
E	There is world-wide co-operation in this project.
F	The problems of noise and air pollution have already been researched.
G	Supersonic jets can fly long distances over Canada and Russia.
H	Concorde is a commercial aircraft.

Question 28

How many countries are involved in developing versions of Concorde II?

*You are advised to spend about 20 minutes on **Questions 29–40** which refer to Reading Passage 3 below.*

READING PASSAGE 3

CO-HOUSING

Co-housing seeks to balance the need for community and privacy in shared living arrangements. The four characteristics essential to co-housing are not new, but the combination is unique to co-housing:

* Participatory process
* Intentional neighbourhood design
* Common facilities
* Resident managed

History
* The first co-housing development was built in Denmark in 1972. The ideas were not entirely new, but interest grew from dissatisfaction with the limited conventional options that were available.
* What we accept as conventional suburbia is not traditional and has really only been with us, or at least regarded as normal, since World War II. It emphasizes privacy at the expense of community, and ownership over access.
* The ubiquitous quarter acre block necessitates car journeys for most basic activities, such as shopping or visiting friends.
* Suburban living is thus an isolating experience for many people; its very structure mitigates against spontaneous casual social interaction.
* House sharing helps promote sharing and a sense of community, but often at the expense of privacy.

The Danish Model
* Co-housing seeks to provide community and privacy in a way that gives people the flexibility to find their own balance and so appeals to a much wider range of people from more diverse backgrounds than house sharing or conventional home ownership.
* Each household has its own dwelling, with bedrooms, bathroom, living and dining areas, and a small kitchen.
* Dwellings are clustered around the common house, with cars kept to the periphery. This type of intentional neighbourhood design is pedestrian friendly and promotes community through increased opportunities for spontaneous social interaction.
* Participatory process is crucial in developing a co-housing project. People get to know one another, and a sense of community grows by working together through the various stages of the development process.
* Resident management means that once different decisions are made, people usually respect them because they had a say. Responsibilities are typically divided among smaller work groups, with all adults participating.

* A range of different ownership structures can be matched with co-housing. Private ownership, rental, and housing co-operatives have all been used in co-housing developments.
* This makes possible a greater range of household types than would otherwise be possible: couples with young children or teenagers, single parents, retired couples and single people. This makes it possible for everyone to have social relationships with people of all ages.
* There are now co-housing communities established right across Europe and in other parts of the world. In size they probably average around thirty households, with some as large as sixty or more, some as small as seven or eight households.

Common House
* The main feature of the common house is the kitchen and dining room. Shared dinners are held there regularly. In some communities that is as few as 2 nights a week, in others up to 7. Everyone takes a turn cooking dinner. Breakfasts and lunches (and dinners when there is no common meal) can be prepared in one's own kitchen and eaten at home or brought to the common house.
* The laundry is the other essential feature of the

community house. Danish communities have found that 2 washing machines and 1 dryer is sufficient for one hundred people.

* There are usually workshops for carpentry/home handy people, car and bicycle maintenance, and textiles. In one community a resident had a pottery workshop in the common house, and in another there was a photography darkroom.

* A casual sitting area near the dining area has been instrumental in the success of some communities.

* A couple of soundproof rooms are also a common inclusion. These can be used as a children's playroom, for music practice, or for teenagers to congregate and make as much noise as they like without disturbing others. Uses for these rooms can change over time as the needs of the community change.

* Some communities have included guest rooms in the common house, which have been quite successful. They can be rented out to visitors, or to teenagers in the community.

Questions 29–32

Answer each of the following questions using **NO MORE THAN TWO WORDS.** The words should be taken **FROM THE TEXT**. Write your answers in the spaces numbered 29–32 on the answer sheet.

29. Write **TWO** characteristics of suburban housing.

30. Write **ONE** negative result of suburban housing.

31. Write **TWO** positive aspects of co-housing.

32. Write **ONE** negative result of house sharing.

Read the following statements **A–G**. Choose the **THREE** statements which reflect a positive outcome of co–housing, according to the section of the text headed **The Danish Model**. Choose the answers **A–G,** and write them in the spaces numbered 33–35 on the answer sheet. You may write them in any order.

A   Privacy is carefully protected.

B   People are not permitted to own cars.

C   The common house is the focus of the community.

D   People respect decisions if they help make them.

E   All adults help to look after the children.

F   People of all ages and interests can interact more.

G   A smaller number of households is better.

Questions 36–40

The following is a summary of the final section of the text, **Common House**. There are some words missing from the summary. From the list of words below, select **ONE** word to fill each space. Write your answers in the spaces numbered 36–40 on the answer sheet.

Summary of Common House

Although each 36. ___household___ has its private 37. ___dwelling___ , everyone shares activities in the common house. The common house might have rooms for cooking and eating or just for sitting and talking. There is usually a common space for washing and drying clothes. Some co-housing projects have special shared rooms for 38. ___hobbies___ such as photography, pottery or for playing 39. ___music___ . This common house gives people of all ages the opportunity to meet each other and socialise. The 40. ___residents___ can make their own decisions on how they use the common space.

List of words

game	household	workshops
hobbies	owner	families
houses	dwelling	practice
residents	children	room
music	activity	family

READING TEST 4

QUESTIONS 1–15

*You are advised to spend about 15 minutes on **Questions 1–15** which refer to Reading Passage 1 below.*

READING PASSAGE 1

???????

A. That 'Monday morning feeling' could be a crushing pain in the chest which leaves you sweating and gasping for breath. Recent research from Germany and Italy shows that heart attacks are more common on Monday mornings and doctors blame the stress of returning to work after the weekend break.

B. The risk of having a heart attack on any given day should be one in seven, but a six-year study coordinated by researchers at the Free University of Berlin of more than 2,600 Germans revealed that the average person had a 20 per cent higher chance of having a heart attack on a Monday than on any other day.

C. Working Germans are particularly vulnerable, with a 33 per cent higher risk at the beginning of the working week. Non-workers, by comparison, appear to be no more at risk on a Monday than any other day.

D. A study of 11,000 Italians identified 8 am on a Monday morning as the most stressful time for the heart, and both studies showed that Sunday is the least stressful day, with fewer heart attacks in both countries.

E. The findings could lead to a better understanding of what triggers heart attacks, according to Dr Stefan Willich of the Free University. 'We know a lot about long-term risk factors such as smoking and cholesterol but we don't know what actually triggers heart attacks, so we can't make specific recommendations about how to prevent them,' he said.

F. Monday mornings have a double helping of stress for the working body as it makes a rapid transition from sleep to activity, and from the relaxing weekend to the pressures of work. 'When people get up, their blood pressure and heart rate go up and there are hormonal changes in their bodies,' Willich explained. 'All these things can have an adverse effect in the blood system and increase the risk of a clot in the arteries which will cause a heart attack. 'When people return to work after a weekend off, the pace of their life changes. They have a higher workload, more stress, more anger and more physical activity,' said Willich. 'We need to know how these events cause changes in the body before we can understand if they cause heart attacks.'

G. But although it is tempting to believe that returning to work increases the risk of a heart attack, both Willich and the Italian researchers admit that it is only a partial answer. Both studies showed that the over–65s are also vulnerable on a Monday morning even though most no longer work. The reason for this is not clear, but the Italian team at the Luigi Saddo Hospital in Milan speculate that social interactions—the thought of facing another week and all its pressures—may play a part.

H. What is clear, however, is that the Monday morning peak seems to be consistent from northern Germany to southern Italy in spite of the differences in diet and lifestyle.

I. Willich is reluctant at this stage to make specific recommendations, but he suggests that anyone who suffers from heart disease should take it easy on Monday mornings and leave potentially stressful meetings until midweek. 'People should try to create a pleasant working environment,' he added. 'Maybe this risk applies only to those who see work as a burden, and people who enjoy their work are not so much at risk. We need to find out more.'

Question 1

Write your answer in the space numbered 1 on the answer sheet.

On which day are people least likely to have a heart attack?

Questions 2–5

Read the following statements 2–5. According to the reading passage, if the statement is true write **T**, if the statement is false write **F**, if there is insufficient evidence write **IE**. Write your answers in the spaces numbered 2–5 on the answer sheet. An example is shown below.

Example:	It was once believed that there was an equal chance of suffering a heart attack on any day of the week.
Answer:	**T**

2. Unemployed Germans have a higher risk of heart attack than employed Germans.

3. Unemployed Italians have a lower risk of heart attack than unemployed Germans.

4. Germans risk heart attack because of their high consumption of fatty food.

5. Cholesterol and smoking cause heart attacks.

Questions 6–14

Read Reading Passage 1 and from the list of headings below, select the best heading for each paragraph **A–I**. Write the appropriate number **i–ix**, in the spaces numbered 6–14 on the answer sheet. Use each heading **ONCE** only.

6. Heading for Paragraph **A**

7. Heading for Paragraph **B**

8. Heading for Paragraph **C**

9. Heading for Paragraph **D**

10. Heading for Paragraph **E**

11. Heading for Paragraph **F**

12. Heading for Paragraph **G**

13. Heading for Paragraph **H**

14. Heading for Paragraph **I**

List of headings

i	Exact cause of heart attacks
ii	The safest day
iii	Breathless, sweaty and crushed
iv	Reducing heart attack hazard
v	High-risk Monday
vi	Mondays: riskier than food and way of life
vii	Jobless but safer
viii	Elderly also at risk
ix	Bodily adaptations

Question 15

Reading Passage 1 is untitled. Select the best title for the entire passage from the choices **A–D** below. Write your answer in space numbered 15 on the answer sheet.

    A   Reduce your chance of having a heart attack

    B   Warning: Mondays are bad for your heart

    C   The overweight and smokers risk heart attacks

    D   Happy and healthy

You are advised to spend about 25 minutes on **Questions 16–28** *which refer to Reading Passage 2 below.*

READING PASSAGE 2

Domestic Division of Labour

Paragraph 1

Work within the family context takes a variety of forms. In many Western households in the 1990s, it may include tasks such as caring for members of the family, contributing to the household finances, maintaining the house, interacting with kin and establishing and sustaining community relationships. As a way of **fostering** domestic harmony and creating a manageable routine, some couples choose one of three different styles of household role division: traditional, egalitarian or collaborative.

Paragraph 2

Most people who fit the traditional pattern are characteristically men and women who are conventionally married, or have been living together as a couple for some time. The man and woman have totally separate spheres of influence and responsibility. For instance, the husband or male partner is usually the chief decision maker and the major financial provider. He brings in the **bulk** of money and has the final say over major household purchases and important financial transactions. The wife or female partner engages in child care and household management, of which the latter also includes maintaining contact with relatives and family members who may not live under the same roof.

Paragraph 3

In ideal situations, an egalitarian style is typified by an equal interchange in household tasks: for example, one partner does the dishes for one week, while the other cooks. Then, the roles are reversed for the next week. As an alternative, individual jobs may be divided equally, so that one partner handles half of the household tasks and the other partner takes on the remaining equal proportion. However, this 50/50 scenario does not usually result in a permanent arrangement, some specialisation does tend to creep in. Human beings are not machines to be switched on and off at precise moments, nor is society organised in such a way as to allow a man to do exactly half the **breadwinning** and a woman to do exactly half the child rearing.

Paragraph 4

The collaborative style is a compromise between the two extremes of traditional and egalitarian. In these families, partners can specialise in household activities and the inclination is towards doing what one is expert at or prefers. Typically, a woman may do all the cleaning while a man may do all the cooking because they choose to do so. It does not follow patriarchal **prescription** where a father always has foremost family authority and where the mother's domain is centred around the children and the household. It is guided by personal interest rather than social convention. As such, decisions may be deferred to the one who is the specialist in the particular area. In some cases, couples may reverse their selected roles and the woman may become the main breadwinner, while the man may in turn be the primary child care-giver.

Paragraph 5

Traditional, egalitarian and collaborative styles are viewed by some as being dependent on female and male gender-role attitudes, both of self and partner. In other words, personality differences are said to determine whether men and women **adopt** one division of labour style in preference to another. Femininity, or female gender-role stereotypes are commonly associated with the emotional, nurturing qualities usually ascribed to a woman, while masculinity, or a male gender-role stereotype is seen in the context of risk-taking, assertiveness and independence— usually attributed to men.

Paragraph 6

An opposing view sees the three family division of labour styles as a reflection of the progressive changes couples make in response to changing life situations, rather than being an aspect of personality. Essentially, adult women and men modify their behaviour within the context of family life, in accordance with current situations. It is these life situations, rather than people, that should be **categorised** as typically feminine or masculine. For example, when a couple begins a loving relationship, attends to a baby or cares for a sick relative, it is the feminine qualities that are foremost. In contrast, competition and the degree of aggressiveness often required in outside employment, are associated with stereotypical masculine qualities.

Paragraph 7

So, depending upon demands in life situations, men and women assign what they believe are the appropriate masculine and feminine characteristics to particular contexts. Moreover, depending upon how **stereotyped** the activities are that they are involved in, gender-roles may alter.

Question 16

In Reading Passage 2, a number of themes are mentioned. From the selection of themes **A– E** below, choose **ONE** which best represents the main theme of the entire passage. Write the appropriate letter in the space numbered 16 on the answer sheet.

List of themes

> **A** home tasks
>
> **B** homework
>
> **C** housework
>
> **D** male and female work
>
> **E** distribution of household tasks

Questions 17–22

Seven sentences have been left out of Reading Passage 2. Each sentence has a **Beginning of Sentence** and an **End of Sentence**. Complete the sentences numbered 17–22 by adding an end of sentence from the selection **A–G** below. Write your answers **A–G** in spaces numbered 17–22 on the answer sheet. The first one has been done as an example.

> *Example:* Examples of Western households ...
>
> *Answer:* **B**

Beginning of Sentence

17. Social scientists ...

18. Role expectations ...

19. Decisions and power within marriage ...

20. In traditional families, males ...

21. Stereotypes ...

22. Males and females ...

End of Sentence

> **A** ... are divided by gender.
>
> **B** ... were considered.
>
> **C** ... are often difficult to change.
>
> **D** ... are often in agreement around the home.
>
> **E** ... and tasks are typically along traditional lines.
>
> **F** ... make the key difference.
>
> **G** ... are divided in their view of what is responsible for the different patterns of domestic division of labour.

Questions 23–28

Paragraphs **2–7** in Reading Passage 2 each contain one word highlighted in bold type. Each highlighted word can be paired with a word of approximately opposite meaning which is in the list **A–N** below. From the list of highlighted words, choose the most suitable opposite meaning. Use each word **ONCE** only. Write your answers in spaces numbered 23–28 on the answer sheet. The first one is an example.

> *Example*:   fostering (Paragraph **1**)
> *Answer*:   **K**

Highlighted words

23. bulk

24. breadwinning

25. prescription

26. adopt

27. categorised

28. stereotyped

Opposite meanings

A differentiated	F choice	K discouraging
B average	G loss	L named
C unclassified	H assume	M outgoings
D owned	I repudiate	N encourage
E minimum	J pattern	

You are advised to spend about 20 minutes on **Questions 29–40** *which refer to Reading Passage 3 below.*

READING PASSAGE 3

The Great Barrier Reef

All along the Queensland coast, inshore coral reefs, smothered by silt and algae, are dying. Some lagoons and reefs, once pristine examples of a tropical paradise, now consist of broken skeletons of dead coral, buried in layers of silt. Even the most remote reefs are at risk of pollution from tourist resorts releasing sewage and ships dumping their rubbish. Tourists too are so numerous that at one popular reef, urine from swimmers, and droppings from fish they feed, have increased the nutrient level in the water so much that algal blooms flourish and threaten the very existence of the colourful corals.

Marine experts say about 70% of coral reefs around the world are dead or severely degraded. Australia's Great Barrier Reef, the globe's largest reef system, stretching 2300 kilometres and comprising 2900 separate reefs, is in better shape than most. But experts warn that it requires concerted effort and diligence to keep it that way and in some places it is already too late.

The Great Barrier Reef is internationally renowned for its spectacular marine life and the tourist and fishing industries are economically important. Reef-based tourism and fishing have a combined economic worth of more than $1 billion a year. Reef tourism is now more valuable than sugar exports and tourist numbers are forecast to quadruple within eight years. The industry depends on protecting a spectacular marine environment that is home to at least 10,000 species of animals (including 400 varieties of coral) and plants. They include such endangered creatures as the dugong, the giant clam and the humpback whale.

It is an environment so little known that thousands more species almost certainly await discovery; during one recent 12 month field study, 200,000 new biological records, information not previously known to science, were made. Many promising compounds for new medical treatments and other products are being discovered on the reef. Compounds derived from sponges and other reef organisms are being evaluated in the United States for possible use in drugs to fight cancer and AIDS. Through newly developing technology, corals are giving us an extraordinary insight into past weather patterns.

Scientists have discovered that long-lived corals on the Great Barrier Reef are vast storehouses of weather information. Over the centuries, corals have absorbed humic acid from plant material washed into the reef from mainland rivers. By examining bands in coral skeletons (analogous to tree rings) under ultraviolet light, scientists have been able to trace rainfall levels back to the 1640s; eventually, they will know what the rainfall was at least 1000 years ago.

Sadly, after several years of research, marine experts agree that inshore reefs are being devastated by a vast deluge of sediment and nutrients washed into the sea as a result of development on the mainland. Some claim that outer reefs will eventually meet the same fate. As internationally renowned marine scientist Leon Zann sums it up: 'It's not the waste on the beaches we have to worry about, it's what we can't see below the surface'.

The reef is being assaulted on other fronts:
• Research suggests that a new invasion of crown-of-thorns starfish, a coral devouring creature, may be imminent. Authorities believe that human activities are implicated in such population explosions.
• Fresh outbreaks of coral bleaching—which occurs when rising temperatures cause polyps to discard the tiny algae that give reefs their colours and which is linked by some scientists to the greenhouse effect, are being recorded.

• Catches of reef fish by commercial and recreational fishermen are falling.

• Ships are illegally discharging oil and dumping garbage; with only one ranger per 5200 square kilometres of the Great Barrier Reef Marine Park, it is difficult to stop them.

• In a controversial move, the oil industry—with the government's blessing—plans to explore waters off the reef for petroleum within the next decade.

Australia is regarded internationally as being in the forefront of reef management and research and is providing $2 million worth of advice on marine issues this year to other countries. Australian scientists have advised Ecuador on how to protect the seas around the famed Galapagos Islands and are helping the Association of South-East Asian Nations to monitor their marine environment, where 80% of reefs are ruined and fish stocks are close to collapse. The hope is that the Great Barrier Reef will avoid a similar fate.

Questions 29–32

Answer the following questions, using information from Reading Passage 3. Select **A, B, C or D** as the best answer and write your answers in the spaces numbered 29–32 on the answer sheet. The first one is an example.

Example:	Queensland is in:
	A Ecuador
	B Austria
	C Australia
	D The United States
Answer:	**C**

29.   The Great Barrier Reef:

   A   has mostly been destroyed

   B   could die in the next decade

   C   is healthier than most other reef systems

   D   is in good condition

30. Corals are scientifically valued because:

    A   they can be made into medicine

    B   they provide shelter for plants

    C   fish feed on them

    D   climatic change is recorded in them

31. Dangers to the marine environment include:

    A   warmer water

    B   coral skeletons

    C   new fish species

    D   high rainfall levels

32. Oil exploration:

    A   has provided an income to the Great Barrier Reef Marine Park

    B   will continue for 10 years

    C   although supported by the government, is not popular

    D   can help scientists monitor marine life

Questions 33–35

The statements below are answers to questions. Choose **ONE** statement from the list labelled **Responses** and match it to the list labelled **Questions**. Write your answers using the appropriate letter from the list of **Responses A–J**, in the spaces numbered 33–35 on the answer sheet. The first one is an example.
There are more responses than you need.

| *Example:* | Where do the biological wastes come from? |
| *Answer:* | **E** |

Questions

33. What causes the most devastation to the coral reefs?

34. Why are scientists still able to make discoveries in the reef system?

35. What is destroying the reefs near the mainland?

Responses

A	sediments and nutrients
B	technology
C	there are too few marine scientists
D	fishing
E	fish and swimmers
F	there are so many marine species
G	it is still largely unexplored
H	damage
I	pollution
J	tourists and ships

Questions 36–38

The following sentence has three words missing. Complete the sentence by adding **ONE** word from Reading Passage 3 for each space. Write your answers in the spaces numbered 36–38 on the answer sheet.

The Great Barrier Reef, the most extensive reef system in the 36. _____ , is important to weather experts who, by studying the structure of 37. _____ , can learn more about amounts of 38. _____ centuries ago.

Questions 39–40

Write your answers in the spaces numbered 39–40 on the answer sheet. Use a maximum of **TWO** words for each answer.

39. Which marine animal is seriously threatening coral?

40. Whose job is it to protect the reef?

READING TEST 5

QUESTIONS 1–15

*You are advised to spend about 15 minutes on **Questions 1–15** which refer to Reading Passage 1 below.*

READING PASSAGE 1

> **WRAP UP YOUR VISIT WITH THE PERFECT GIFT**

Section 1A

'It is better to give than to receive'; 'Never look a gift horse in the mouth'; Beware of Greeks (ancient, of course) bearing gifts'. Gifts are a fundamental element of culture and our lives as social creatures. They are also an important part of our business relationships.

There are occasions when giving a gift surpasses spoken communication, since the message it offers can cut through barriers of language and cultural diversity. Present a simple gift to your host in a foreign country and the chances are he or she will understand you perfectly, though you may not understand a single word of each other's languages. It can convey a wealth of meaning about your appreciation of their hospitality and the importance you place upon the relationship.

Combine the act of giving with some knowledge of and sensitivity to the culture of the recipient and you have an invaluable chance to earn respect and lay the foundations of a durable and mutually beneficial business relationship.

For all countries, take account of climate, especially in regard to clothing. Some gifts can be ruined by extremely hot or humid climates, possibly causing their receiver considerable anguish. Consider the kinds of products that are abundant in the country concerned and try for something that is uncommon there. Think about the level of language skills: a book with hundreds of pages of English text may be at best useless, at worst embarrassing, to a person with limited English. Inform yourself as much as possible about local customs, rules and etiquette, especially to do with wrapping, presenting, superstitions, taboos and, importantly, customs and quarantine regulations. The following is a brief account of the etiquette of gift-giving in some countries of Asia and the Middle East.

Section 1B

Hong Kong Chinese greatly appreciate simple greeting cards, though obviously they will not refuse small tokens of friendship in the form of gifts.

Books with plenty of illustrations are most appreciated in Indonesia. Inappropriate items: alcohol, products made from pigs, warm clothing. Ties and cuff links are not commonly worn.

In Iran, short-sleeved shirts and any visual representation of naked or partially dressed people, male or female are highly inappropriate. Don't bother with ties, videos or records. As in all Islamic countries, there is a strict taboo on any pork products.

Respecting the Arab tradition, gifts should endeavour to praise the recipient in Iraq and should never be of an order that cannot reasonably be reciprocated.

Avoid certain colour combinations: red, white and black (colours of the Nazi flag); and red, green and black (the Palestinian flag) in Israel.

Gifts are normally exchanged at the beginning of meetings with Japanese and should be given and received with both hands. It is seen as impolite to give an unwrapped gift. The emphasis should be on high quality, though not necessarily expensive, items.

When in Jordan, it is preferable, but not vital, to avoid green in packaging. Do not give books, videos, etc that mention Israel. Normal Arab customs apply, so no alcohol, pork, women's clothing etc. Arabs generally do not greatly appreciate handcrafts in wood, fabric or pottery. Gifts should ideally appear valuable.

Again, the exchange should be made with both hands in Korea. Also, similar to Japan, is the emphasis on presentation. Do not use red ink to write the names of the recipients. It is worth remembering that it is customary for a gift given to a company to be shared out around the office concerned, so items that lend themselves to this practice—like a bottle of good whisky—are very well received.

Laos has virtually no cultural taboo items. It would be difficult to offend with virtually any gift.

Business contacts in the People's Republic of China are keen recipients of good Scotch whisky and American cigarettes, to the point where it is almost obligatory to take some along when you go there. Or, if not obligatory, it certainly helps to warm relations.

Do not open gifts in the presence of the giver in the Philippines. Not recommended are items alluding to religion. Many people are Catholic and many others Moslems. This also means literature and art with any possible suggestions of lewdness or racism are to be strictly avoided.

For Thailand, gifts should not be wrapped or packaged in black. Modest gifts, like ties, scarves and key rings, are much appreciated. Traditionally, sharp objects like knives or even letter openers are not given as gifts.

No special gift-giving customs in Vietnam, but the Vietnamese are enthusiastic gift givers and like very much to receive them as well. Liquor and wine can be problematic, for reasons pertaining to Vietnamese tastes rather than morality or religion.

Questions 1–4

Statements 1–4 are based on Reading Passage 1. Complete the statements by using **ONE** word from Reading Passage 1 for each answer. Write your answers in the spaces numbered 1–4 on the answer sheet.

1. Differences in culture and _____ can be overcome by gifts.

2. Overseas visitors are advised to give gifts to their _____ .

3. _____ should be considered when giving gifts such as thick clothing.

4. To present a gift of chocolates in a tropical country might create _____ .

Read each of the following statements. Write **T** if the statement is true, **F** if the statement is false and **IE** if there is insufficient evidence, according to Reading Passage 1. Write your answers in the spaces numbered 5–10 on the answer sheet.

5.   An Israeli business manager would undoubtedly appreciate the gift of a black, white and red striped tie.

6.   It is recommended to give wine to Vietnamese.

7.   An inexpensive pigskin wallet would probably be appreciated in Japan, Vietnam and Laos.

8.   A silk scarf is an appropriate gift for a Jordanian host's wife.

9.   Umbrellas are popular gifts in Hong Kong.

10.   Whisky would be a welcome gift in Laos.

Questions 11–15

The paragraph below is a summary based on information in Reading Passage 1. There are some words missing. Complete the paragraph by using **ONE** word for each space. All the words you will need to use come from Reading Passage 1. Write your answers in the spaces numbered 11–15 on the answer sheet.

There are important details to consider when 11. _____ . Some cultures have prohibitions on animal products such as those from a 12. _____ . Others have political aversions to specific 13. _____ because of their use on certain countries' flags. Similarly, Thais do not like 14. _____ covered gifts, and in Korea it is suggested that name tags written in red should be avoided. But presentation is not only restricted to what wrapping or pen you use, in Japan care should also be taken in selecting gifts that are of superior 15. _____ .

You are advised to spend about 20 minutes on **Questions 16–25** *which refer to Reading Passage 2 below.*

READING PASSAGE 2

EARTHQUAKE

A. Earthquakes can rip apart entire cities and outlying districts, as the 1995 disaster in Kobe, Japan showed. Seismologists, scientists who study earthquakes and related phenomena, have records dating back to 1556, from the Chinese province of Shensi, which indicate that earthquakes have been devastating our world for centuries. In that instance, a major earthquake is estimated to have killed nearly 830,000 people, while destroying whole towns and villages. More recently, a death toll of more than 66,000 was recorded in northern Peru in 1970, and 23,000 died in the Guatemala quake of 1976.

B. The destructive forces which produce earthquakes, usually begin deep below the ground, along a fault in weaker areas of the earth's rocky outer shell, where sections of rock repeatedly slide past each other. The speed at which the fracture spreads at point of weakness depends upon the type of rock but may average about 3 km a second in granite or other strong rock. At that rate, a fracture may spread more than 560 km in one direction in less than a minute. As the fracture extends along the fault, blocks of rock on one side of the fault may drop down below the rock on the other side, move up and over the other side, or slide forward past the other. The violent shattering of rock releases energy that travels in waves, and these seismic waves move out from the focus of the earthquake in all directions. As the waves travel away from the focus, they grow gradually weaker, generally resulting in the ground shaking less as distances increase.

C. Geological movements are not the only occurrences to trigger an earthquake. Human activity, most often the filling of reservoirs with extraordinarily large amounts of water, can also cause earthquakes. Lake Mead, on the Colorado River in the United States, was filled in 1935 and was the first example of an artificial lake being responsible for earthquake activity. Similarly, massive explosions, such as quarry blasting and nuclear tests can also wreak havoc.

D. Earthquakes almost never kill people directly, although that fact is not of much consolation to relatives and friends who have lost loved ones in an earthquake. Instead, many deaths and injuries result from falling objects and collapsing buildings, while fire resulting from broken gas or fallen power lines is another danger. The Kobe earthquake in January 1995, lasted only 20 seconds, yet resulted in a death toll of over 5,000 and injured approximately 26,000 people. Fires burnt out of control for several days after the earthquake, which was followed by hundreds of after-shocks. Because of fears of damage to gas pipelines and any leaks being potentially disastrous, inhabitants endured freezing winter conditions.

E. Even though earthquake prone countries spend enormous human and financial resources on seismographic measurement, as a means of predicting earthquakes, there is a danger in paying too much heed to seemingly high risk zones and erecting less stable buildings solely because of their being in a low risk zone. Prior to the earthquake, Kobe was not regarded as at serious risk, but after the disaster, investigation of the damage revealed that nearly all deaths occurred in small buildings that shattered rather than twisted when stressed. Coupled with the problem of soft soils, the buildings had little firm support and many crumbled. If countries wish to withstand the devastating forces of substantial earthquakes and reduce death, injury and property damage, it is important to design and construct buildings that are earthquake resistant, as well as monitor seismic forces.

Questions 16–18

Select words from paragraph **B** to answer Questions 16–18. Use **ONE** word for each answer. Write your answers in the spaces numbered 16–18 on the answer sheet.

16. Name the precondition needed in rock for below surface fractures to occur.

17. Which term is used for the location of the greatest amount of movement?

18. What action below the surface rock results in seismic waves?

Questions 19–22

The notes below are a summary of paragraph **C** of Reading Passage 2. Choose words from paragraph **C** to complete the notes and write your answers in the spaces numbered 19–22. Select either **ONE** or **TWO** words for each space.

Both natural and 19. _____ activity can cause an 20. _____ .

21. _____ formation of lakes by discharge of 22. _____ can initiate a quake.

Questions 23–25

Write the appropriate letter **A, B, C** or **D** in the spaces numbered 23–25 on the answer sheet.

23. It is now believed that:

   A low-risk zones are relatively safe.

   B high-risk zones are more dangerous than low-risk zones.

   C low-risk zones may in fact be very dangerous due to poorly constructed buildings.

   D high-risk zones have stable buildings.

24. Soft soils:

   A together with poorly constructed buildings and being in high-risk zones greatly contribute to earthquake devastation.

   B cause earthquakes.

   C cause buildings to twist rather than shatter.

   D crumble buildings.

25. Seismologists:

A can predict the potential destruction of a city by an earthquake.

B cannot predict where an earthquake may occur.

C had been investigating Kobe's potential for an earthquake and had warned the inhabitants.

D could work with other professionals to understand and try to minimise the level of death and injury caused by major earthquakes.

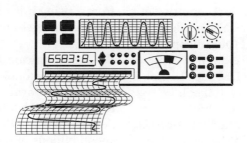

*You are advised to spend about 25 minutes on **Questions 26–40** which refer to Reading Passage 3 below.*

READING PASSAGE 3

WHY WE CAN'T AFFORD TO LET ASIA STARVE

A. Among the problems afflicting a burgeoning world population, overcrowding, poverty and environmental degradation are combining to put at risk the very essence of our survival—food.

B. 'If by the beginning of the next century we have failed to satisfy the very basic needs of the two billion very poor and four billion poor, life for the rest of us could be extremely risky and uncomfortable,' predicts Dr Klaus Lampe of the International Rice Research Institute (IRRI) in the Philippines. This is a highly threatening, even terrifying prediction for Asia, where 70 per cent of the world's poor live but where reserves of good quality arable land have practically run out.

C. Although the world regards Asia as the focus of an economic and industrial miracle, without adequate supplies of food, Lampe says, chaos could easily result in many countries. And the impact will be felt widely throughout the region. In the 1990s alone, he says, the cities of Asia will be swollen by a further 500 million people—nearly equal to the population of the United States and European Community combined. 'The only growing population in Asia is that of the poor. Prime productive land is being used for city expansion and building roads, while thousands of hectares are being taken out of production each year because of salinity or alkalinity.'

D. From the mid-1960s when the Green Revolution began, Asian food production doubled through a combination of high-yielding crops, expanded farming area and greater intensification. From now on, growing enough food will depend almost entirely on increasing yield from the same, or smaller, area of land. However, a mysterious threat is emerging in the noticeably declining yields of rice from areas that have been most intensively farmed. Unless scientists can unravel why this is so, food output in Asia may actually stagnate at a time when population will double.

E. Such issues, Lampe argues, while seen as remote by many countries and international corporations, will strike at their economic base as well. Societies that are too poor or driven by internal strife and civil war will be bad for investment or as markets for goods. Pressure from a rising tide of environmental and political refugees may also be felt.

F. One significant factor undermining the agricultural economies of developing countries has been the farm trade war between the US and the EC. 'We talk about environmental degradation and dangerous chemicals, yet spend billions of US dollars and ECUs producing things we don't want which ruin local production systems and incomes for poor people,' Lampe says. And instead of developed countries helping struggling nations to develop sustainable food production systems, their policies tend to erode and destroy them.

G. When world grain prices are bad, farmers in Asia's uplands turn from rice to cash crops to supplement falling incomes, or clear larger areas of rainforest with catastrophic environmental consequences within just a few years. Cleared rainforest soils are highly erosive; even where they are not, they rapidly become acid and toxic under intense cultivation and plants die, forcing the clearing of ever-larger areas.

H. Research at the IRRI has indicated that intensive rice production—growing two or three crops a year on the same land—is showing signs of yield declines as great as 30 per cent. Evidence for this comes from as far afield as India, The Philippines and Indonesia. At the same time, agricultural research worldwide has been contracting as governments, non-government bodies and private donors reduce funding because of domestic economic pressures. This means, Lampe says, that at risk is the capacity to solve such problems as rice yield decline and research to breed the new generation of super-yielding crops. Yet rice will be needed to feed more than half the human population—an estimated 4.5 billion out of 8.3 billion people by 2030.

I. Compared with the building of weapons of mass destruction or the mounting of space missions to Mars, Lampe says, the devising of sustainable farming systems has little political appeal to most governments: 'To them I say: I hope you can sleep well at night.'

Questions 26–33

Reading Passage 3 has 9 paragraphs. Choose the most suitable heading for each paragraph from the list **i–xii** below. Use each heading **ONCE** only. Write your answers in the spaces 26–33 on the answer sheet. The first one is an example. **There are more headings than paragraphs, so you won't use all the headings.**

Example:	Paragraph **A**.
Answer:	**iv**

26. Paragraph **B**

27. Paragraph **C**

28. Paragraph **D**

29. Paragraph **E**

30. Paragraph **F**

31. Paragraph **G**

32. Paragraph **H**

33. Paragraph **I**

List of Headings

i	Decrease in food yields
ii	Drop in yield affected by reduction in research
iii	Pollution ruining crops
iv	World at risk due to predicted food shortage
v	Lack of international interest
vi	Bid to retrain Asian farmers
vii	Desperate situation for Asia
viii	Environmental degradation due to changed farming methods
ix	Need to increase soil fertility
x	Population explosion compounds Asia's problems
xi	International commerce threatens Asian agriculture
xii	Food shortages have wide effects

Questions 34–35

Name **TWO** reasons for loss of farm land. Use a maximum of **TWO** words in both of your answers. Write your answers in spaces 34–35 on the answer sheet.

Questions 36–40

The flow chart below describes some consequences of Asian agriculture. Each step follows the previous step, forming a chain of consequences. Complete the flow chart by selecting the appropriate letter from the list of consequences below, to fill spaces numbered 36–40 on the answer sheet.
Some letters may be used more than once.

```
┌────────────────────────────┐
│       Example:  C          │
└────────────────────────────┘
              ⇩
┌────────────────────────────┐
│           36.              │
└────────────────────────────┘
              ⇩
┌────────────────────────────┐
│           37.              │
└────────────────────────────┘
              ⇩
┌────────────────────────────┐
│           38.              │
└────────────────────────────┘
              ⇩
┌────────────────────────────┐
│           39.              │
└────────────────────────────┘
              ⇩
┌────────────────────────────┐
│           40.              │
└────────────────────────────┘
```

Consequences

A vegetation destroyed	**D** rainforest cleared
B need to supplement income	**E** acid soil
C poor world grain price	

READING TEST 6

*You are advised to spend about 20 minutes on **Questions 1–14** which refer to Reading Passage 1 below.*

READING PASSAGE 1

INTELLECTUAL DISABILITY

A. People with intellectual disability form one of the largest single disability groups in a community. Intellectual disability refers to a general slowness to learn and function within society, and the identification of intellectual disability is usually based on an assessment of a person's performance in a variety of tests. An individual's level of performance, as assessed, can change with time and circumstances. On occasions, an intellectually disabled person may perform better than at other times. Evidence for this inconsistent level of performance comes from modern research and practice which have shown that with skilled training and opportunity for development, people with intellectual disability have much greater potential for acquiring skills and for participation in community life than previously had been thought possible.

B. In many western societies, five categories of intellectual disability have traditionally been used in order to indicate the perceived degree of difficulty an individual has with learning. All five may occur in either children, adolescents or adults, and show as mild, moderate, severe, profound or multiple intellectual disability. However, undue reliance on such categories and the consequent 'pigeonholing' of individuals into one of the five categories can result in failure to provide the opportunities for each person to develop.

C. For the majority of intellectual disabilities, there is no identifiable cause but there are some causes that are well documented. They include: brain damage at birth due to lack of oxygen—prolonged labour during childbirth; brain damage before birth due to factors such as rubella, drug or diet-related problems; damage after birth due to illnesses such as encephalitis or accidents; hereditary defects in the genes; abnormal chromosome count resulting in, for example, Down Syndrome.

D. Like everyone else, people with an intellectual disability need a rewarding job, a satisfying place to live and a good social life. But they may need extra support to achieve these things. Good support services are based on the principle of normalisation—which means enabling people to be part of the community like everyone else. In turn, normalisation needs to be well-integrated into the community, in order to be effective. Some of the services needed include assessment centres, training for employment and support to keep jobs once they get them, residential accommodation that is homelike. For children, early education and school education appropriate to the child's needs, are essential. Without a strong community-based system of care, the intellectually disabled run the risk of becoming a huge underclass as in the United States, where thousands of intellectually disabled are homeless because of the American policy of de-institutionalisation.

E. With the introduction of the intellectually disabled into communities, there is a need to promote awareness of communication. Although many people may have little experience in talking with an intellectually disabled person, and anticipate great difficulty in communication, there are common guidelines that can simplify the interaction. Firstly, it is useful to remember that people with disabilities have feelings and can usually understand what is said, even though they sometimes may take longer to respond. Speaking in the same friendly manner as you would to anyone else, and using straightforward language and uncomplicated sentences, is also recommended. Being prepared to wait a little longer for replies during a conversation with an intellectually disabled person, would undoubtedly benefit the exchange. Above all, it is suggested not to talk about the person with someone else within their hearing. Ultimately, the idea is to encourage intellectually disabled people to do things for themselves.

Questions 1–3

Complete the following statements by writing **ONE** word from Reading Passage 2 in the spaces numbered 1–3 on the answer sheet.

1. Training helps intellectually disabled people be a part of a _____ .

2. In order to retain a job people with disabilities need _____ .

3. Housing for intellectually disabled people needs to be _____ .

Questions 4–8

Read each statement and according to the text, write **T** if the statement is true, **F** if the statement is false and **IE** of there is insufficient evidence. Write your answers in the spaces numbered 4–8 on the answer sheet.

4. Intellectual disability is an unchanging disorder.

5. Poor nutrition in mothers can lead to brain damage in newborns.

6. Down syndrome is the result of a shortage of oxygen at birth.

7. Work is the most urgent need for a person with disabilities.

8. Intellectually disabled people usually have hearing problems.

Questions 9–10

According to Reading Passage 1, which **TWO** causes of brain damage are not related to birth or genes. Use **ONE** word for each answer. Write your answers in the spaces numbered 9–10 on the answer sheet.

Questions 11–14

Select the best heading from the list below for each paragraph **A–E** in Reading Passage 1. Use each letter **ONCE** only. Write the appropriate letter **A–E**, in the spaces numbered 11–14 on the answer sheet.
There are more headings than paragraphs, so you won't use all of the headings.

Example:	Paragraph **A**
Answer:	**iii**

11. Paragraph **B**

12. Paragraph **C**

13. Paragraph **D**

14. Paragraph **E**

List of Headings

i	How is intellectual disability assessed?
ii	What do people with an intellectual disability need?
iii	What is intellectual disability?
iv	How do people with an intellectual disability talk?
v	What are the forms of intellectual disability?
vi	What causes intellectual disability?
vii	How do you talk to a person with an intellectual disability?
viii	Which community-based intellectual disability services are available?

You are advised to spend about 15 minutes on **Questions 15–24** which refer to Reading Passage 2 below.

READING PASSAGE 2

Fuel Cells: 21st Century Electricity

The 21st century's leading energy source may very well depend on the development of a technology that was first discovered in 1839. Indeed, many experts believe that the future of electricity generation will not come from further refinement of solar, wind, coal or nuclear energy, but from fuel cells. Among the various types of fuel cells, the ceramic or solid oxide fuel cell promises to achieve the greatest efficiency of conversion of fossil fuels such as gas and coal to electricity while producing only very low levels of pollutants. To this end, a consortium comprising five leading organisations has established Ceramic Fuels Ltd, initially to expand fuel cell research and development and secondly, to bring the technology to commercial application.

Ceramic fuel cells are electrochemical devices that directly convert fuels such as gasified coal or natural gas into electricity without the limitation of the Carnot cycle (an ideal thermodynamic cycle in which heat is taken onto a working fluid at a constant upper temperature and rejected at a constant lower temperature). In many respects, fuel cells work like batteries. As long as they are constantly supplied with fuel and oxidant, fuel cells can continuously produce power, removing the need for recharging.

Fuel cells offer several advantages over traditional thermal power plants. The major difference between these two power generators is that the chemical energy of the fuel cell is converted directly to electrical power without intermediate conversion first to heat. The efficiency of a coal-fired thermal plant is typically in the range of 30%–35%. In a combined cycle gas turbine system running on natural gas, the maximum efficiency is in the range 45%–50%. Many experts believe high temperature fuel cells could reach efficiencies of 80%–85%. Ceramic fuel cells thus offer a more efficient and less polluting alternative to current power generation technologies.

By-products from fuel cells are high quality heat, carbon dioxide and steam. The temperature of the exhaust gases is well above 500° C, meaning that solid oxide fuel cells are very attractive for electricity and heat generation as, in addition to supplying electricity, the leftover amounts of heat created during the process could be used to produce heat for industries, provide hot water supplies or warm buildings.

Fuel cell technology is not new. In fact, the principles of fuel cell operation were first reported by British scientist Sir William Grove in 1839. His prototype used dilute sulphuric acid and operated at room temperature. Ceramic fuel cells developed much later, with the first one operating at 1000° C in 1937.

Ceramic fuel cells offer many advantages over other energy systems:

- they have the potential to produce electricity efficiently from several fuel sources
- they can generate large amounts of electricity
- they are relatively quick to install

Fuel cell research and development is extremely competitive worldwide, with the USA, Japan and some European countries leading the charge to commercialise this promising technology. For instance, a Dutch-Belgian company has developed a fuel cell for a Volkswagen van and is also working on a larger unit to power a bus. Additionally, a German company is working on a fuel cell for the European space shuttle program and for submarines, while a Canadian company is evaluating a fuel cell to be used in small buses.

Recent reports point to promising large international markets for ceramic fuel cells. Prospects for fuel cells in South East Asian markets appear good. Several countries, including Indonesia, Thailand and The

Philippines, are expected to demonstrate high rates of growth in demand for power, an encouraging situation for those countries quick enough to develop and commercialise fuel cell technology.

Energy is a vital component of a technology-based society, and the growing need for electricity generation by the most efficient method will ensure a promising future for ceramic fuel cell technology. The Ceramic Fuel Cells Ltd initiative represents a major collaborative venture between public and private sectors. It is envisaged that this venture will go a long way towards achieving a greater efficiency of energy use worldwide.

Questions 15–19

Use a maximum of **TWO** words from the reading passage to answer each of questions 15–19. Write your answers in spaces numbered 15–19 on the answer sheet.

15. Which group has predicted a significant change in future energy generation?
16. Fuel cells are positive for the environment because they release minimal amounts of which substances?
17. Which common energy sources have been compared to fuel cells?
18. What is the potential percentage gain in efficiency when comparing old style energy generators and fuel cells?
19. When were ceramic fuel cells first used?

Questions 20–24

Decide whether the statements below support information in Reading Passage 2. In the spaces numbered 20–24 on the answer sheet, write:

Yes	if the statements support information
No	if the statements do not support information
Not Given	if the statements do not refer to information

An example has been done for you.

| *Example:* | Sir William Grove was a physicist. |
| *Answer:* | **Not Given** |

20. Future transport vehicles may be powered by fuel cells.
21. European companies were first in the race to develop fuel cell technology.
22. Some rapidly developing South East Asian countries will soon market fuel cells.
23. Indonesia has an enormous need for fossil fuels.
24. Cooperation between private companies and governments will encourage wider use of efficient energy sources.

You are advised to spend about 25 minutes on **Questions 25–40** *which refer to Reading Passage 3 below.*

READING PASSAGE 3

The New Ice Age

Antarctica's long dark winter evokes visions of early explorers barely surviving in huts, their huskies and sleds snowbound outside in the harshest conditions imaginable. But times have changed.

Although expeditioners like Mawson, Scott and Amundsen explored and wintered on the continent in the early years of the century, the notion of operating permanent year-round bases in Antarctica was relatively new until the 1950s and 1960s. Even after the Second World War, Antarctica was still being opened up and there were many blank spots on the map. Mawson station, opened in 1954, and Davis in 1957 are Australia's two oldest, continually operated bases on the continent.

In the past, life at these bases was hardly luxurious. It meant camping in cramped zinc-alum sheds, listening to katabatic winds scream in the long winter night. Communication with the outside world was restricted to just a few telegraphed lines. Expeditioners heading south were issued with pamphlets listing five-letter codes covering almost every conceivable situation so they could communicate with their families and still keep within strict 'word limits' during their year on base. Humour boosted morale and was an important element of life there. For instance 'YIKLA' was code for 'This is the life!'

Today, living year-round in Antarctica is considerably easier. The weather hasn't changed of course, but you can pick up a telephone and dial direct anywhere in the world. The cost is very modest and is subsidised at 90 cents a minute. All that individuals need to do is to collect the bill at the end of the year.

Because the summer-time work of scientists tends to capture the public's imagination, with revelations about the ozone hole or whale numbers, people tend to overlook the efforts of the 20 or so winterers at each base—mostly tradespeople—who keep the bases going long after 'the boffins' (research scientists) have migrated to warmer climates. In doing so, they also keep alive claims to sovereignty of sections of the continent and maintain their environmental interest in this sensitive part of the planet. Aside from its wealth of marine resources, Antarctica controls much of the southern hemisphere's climate. As the only other wholly southern hemisphere continent, Australia, more than any other large nation, has the most at stake in what happens here.

So what is life like down there? Over the past year, wintering on an Antarctic base has become positively civilised. The conclusion last summer of a 10-year building program has seen the historic zinc-alum shacks and even older wooden sheds built at an early Antarctic base, on Heard Island in 1947, supplanted by vast, bright-coloured buildings with bay-window views and ski-lodge decor. There are video lounges, gymnasiums, bars and libraries. The workshops are comparable to anything in modern industrialised countries. The food is plentiful. There are even field huts that double as weekenders for those who feel the need to get away from it all. The money's good and everything from beer to socks is supplied free. Not everyone is pleased with the new luxury. Nowhere were the changes felt more keenly than at Mawson, where the old quarters, with their rugged outpost atmosphere, were shut and the last team of huskies removed. To many old Antarctic hands, it marked the end of the great 'Intrepid Age' in Antarctica.

There are some things about life in Antarctica, however, that even central heating and watching a live-via-satellite sports broadcast cannot change. The Antarctic Territory is still one of the most exotic places on Earth. Few people will ever get there. There are no flights which land there—you have to travel as the early explorers did, almost a century ago, by sea. Going to Mawson, for example, means a two-week voyage on an icebreaker such as *Aurora Australis*, across 5000 kilometres of the Southern Ocean, one of the roughest stretches of water on Earth. Waves can exceed 15 metres, the ship can pitch 40 degrees and, if you're not a good sailor, even the industrial strength Avomine prescribed by Antarctic Division doctors won't keep breakfast down. Most often though, tourist ships sail from South American ports, which offer the easiest access to the spectacular coastal scenery of the Antarctic Peninsula.

Once there, after the short shipping season has ended, some time in February when the ice closes in, there is no changing your mind and heading home. You are there for the duration, at least until the pack ice breaks up the following November. Like the early explorers, you are confronted with the challenge of getting along with a small, isolated group of people through the long winter night. Learning to put up with their foibles the way they have to put up with yours. Which is why everyone applying for a job in Antarctica is interviewed by a psychologist before being accepted. As one veteran diesel mechanic at Davis put it: 'If you make an ass of yourself down here, there's no place you can go.'

Questions 25–29

The paragraph below summarises information from Reading Passage 3. Select **ONE** word from the reading passage to fill each gap. Write your answers in the spaces numbered 25–29 on the answer sheet.

Antarctica in the 1950s was a very different place from the Antarctica of the 1990s. In those early days, 25. _____ was limited but today, with advancements in telecommunications, 26. _____ calls are not only convenient, they are quite cheap. But however much life in Antarctica improves to become more 27. _____ in terms of facilities, accommodation and food, the 28. _____ never changes. Because of this, scientists, tradespeople, or tourists cannot travel out of Antarctica until at least 29. _____ .

Write the appropriate letter **A**, **B**, **C** or **D** in the spaces numbered 30–33 on the answer sheet.

30. The early Antarctic explorers:

    A   travelled to the continent during winter.

    B   first explored Antarctica in the 1950s.

    C   opened permanent bases in Antarctica.

    D   were isolated by heavy snow falls.

31. Those currently employed in Antarctica:

    A   work only in summer.

    B   maintain permanent all season bases.

    C   are all publicly acknowledged.

    D   are all scientists studying the environment.

32. Recreational opportunities include:

    A   staying in short term holiday huts.

    B   working in modern workshops.

    C   relaxing in ski lodges.

    D   sailing to South America.

33. The closure of Mawson base:

    A   caused many explorers to leave Antarctica.

    B   occurred in 1995.

    C   symbolised the change to modern working conditions.

    D   was welcomed by experienced Antarctic explorers.

Five sentences have been left out of Reading Passage 3. Each sentence is divided into **Beginning of Sentence** and **End of Sentence**. Complete questions 34–37 by adding a phrase from **A–E**. Write your answers in the spaces numbered 34–37 on the answer sheet.

Example:	All workers ...
Answer:	**B**

Beginning of Sentence

34. A major problem is to ...

35. Expeditioners learn ...

36. The pre-departure programs ...

37. Long-term Antarctic residents learn ...

End of Sentence

A   ... concentrate on the vital aspects of living in a small, isolated community.

B   ... undertake intensive training before going to Antarctica.

C   ... stay through winter with no physical contact with the outside world.

D   ... to survive in freezing conditions, emergency rescue procedures, mountain climbing, radio communications and vehicle use and care.

E   ... to wait until summer for mail from home.

Questions 38–40

In Reading Passage 3 a number of difficulties and their solutions are mentioned. Answer uestions 38–40 by listing a solution for each difficulty. Use **ONE** word for each solution. All the words you use will come from Reading Passage 3. Write your solutions in the spaces numbered 38–40 on the answer sheet.

38. low spirits of the early expeditioners

39. seasickness

40. how to check the personality of an Antarctic job-seeker

READING TEST 7

QUESTIONS 1–14

*You are advised to spend about 20 minutes on **Questions 1–14** which refer to Reading Passage 1 below.*

READING PASSAGE 1

TOOLS FOR TOMORROW'S TELECOMMUNICATIONS

For some time yet, much of our telecommunicating will continue to depend on the existing web of thin copper wires that telephonically link most of our homes and workplaces. Making it possible for that network to match the communications demands of the near future will require new technologies that widen the lanes on the information highway.

The standard telephone service is something we take for granted in today's modern world. The public telecommunications network provides a reliable and highly accessible service—we have high expectations and react strongly when the service is unavailable. To meet the demand for high reliability, and to provide services economically, the public network is being progressively upgraded.

Yet consumers are still waiting for the widespread use of new services such as the video phone, which was first demonstrated 30 years ago. What then is required to make new services such as video telecommunications possible and widely available? Apart from the availability of inexpensive video terminal equipment, the key requirement is increased bandwidth (that is, more available frequencies for transmission) which must be provided by the network at an affordable cost. Understanding how this objective might be achieved requires a review of the existing telecommunications network and the new technologies that are expected to improve and extend its capacity.

The traditional telephone network consists of a pair of copper wires connecting the customer premises to a local exchange. This is known as the customer access network. The local exchange is connected to other local exchanges through a series of intermediate exchanges, using coaxial cable, microwave or satellite transmission links. This part of the network is referred to as the core network. Within the core network, a technique known as multiplexing is used so only a small number of physical connections are needed between each telephone exchange. As a result, each transmission link may carry thousands of telephone conversations simultaneously.

Traditionally the telephone network used analogue switching and transmission techniques. Since the 1970s, the core network has been progressively changed from an analogue to a digital network. Digital technology offers better quality, with the capability to actively regenerate the original transmitted signal even when buried in unwanted noise. Pulse Code Modulation (PCM) is the process in which the analogue telephone signal is converted to a digital one. Each analogue voice signal is sampled at a rate of 8000 times a second, with one sample represented by eight bits of digital information. Each voice signal therefore requires a 64 kilobits/second transmission channel.

The physical connections in the core network have in recent years been changed to fibre optic cable. A large fibre optic network can connect many major metropolitan centres. Fibre optic cable is fundamentally the most important transmission technology because of the high bandwidth that it offers.

The shift from the analogue to digital world within the core network exchanges means that a majority of local exchanges are now digital exchanges. What then of the customer access network? A long term goal is to upgrade the customer access network using fibre optic cable, which will allow the delivery of new high bandwidth services such as video-on-demand. However, this final step from the local exchange to the customer is an expensive one, due to the large number of connections involved. Only when the demand for these new services is well established can the cost of large scale deployment of fibre optic cable in the customer network be justified.

Questions 1–4

Answer the following questions with **NOT MORE THAN THREE** words which **MUST COME FROM THE TEXT.** Write your answers in spaces numbered 1–4 on the answer sheet.

1.   What does today's telecommunicating depend on?

2.   What are the words used to describe today's standard telephone service?

3–4. What are **TWO** main requirements to make new services accessible?

Questions 5–8

Decide which of the following statements according to the text are true **T**, false **F** or for which there is insufficient evidence **IE** and write **T**, **F** or **IE** in the spaces numbered 5–8 on the answer sheet.

5.   The customer access network does not include any physical connections.

6.   Multiplexing reduces the need for numerous physical links between exchanges.

7.   There are three main ways of making connections across the core network.

8.   There is a limit to the number of telephone conversations that may take place at any given time.

Questions 9–14

Decide which of the following features refer to present, past (traditional) or future technology and write **P** for present, **T** for past (traditional) or **F** for future in spaces numbered 9–14 on your answer sheet. One has been done for you as an example.

Example:	64 bits/sec transmission channel
Answer:	**P**

9.   video on demand

10.   analogue transmission

11.   Pulse Code Modulation

12.   fibre optic cable in core network

13.   digital exchange

14.   use of fibre optic cable in customer access network

You are advised to spend about 20 minutes on **Questions 15–27** *which refer to Reading Passage 2 below.*

READING PASSAGE 2

Characteristics of Open and Distance Learning

A _____

Open learning is generally seen as a goal of education, characterised by increasing flexibility of methodological and administrative practices in the interests of maximising the options and support available for students. Distance teaching is characterised by four things: 1) the need to individualise learning, 2) the use of a range of teaching and supervisory strategies which are not primarily face-to-face, 3) the need to determine, in advance of teaching, the activities, interactions and resources necessary to achieve the purposes of a course unit or subject, and 4) an openness to the educational possibilities afforded by developments in computer and communications technologies.

B _____

The major educational distinction between on-campus and distance teaching is the reliance on group-based strategies in the former and the obligation to individualise instruction in the latter. These individualised strategies also need to be supported by a compatible administrative system. For academics whose experience is primarily of study on-campus, there is some challenge in distance education, because the assumptions which underpin individualised learning may be quite different from those with which they are familiar. The Distance Education Centre provides support to academics who are teaching students at a distance with the aim of helping them understand the different demands of this kind of teaching.

C _____

Major differences between the teaching modes result from the following factors:
* the logistics of communication
* the degree to which the lecturer is able to respond to student input
* the role of peer-group influence
* student access to learning resources

* the complexity of the administrative arrangements which support the learning program
* the extent to which the lecturer can influence the learning environment of the student.

The university believes that good teaching requires that these distinctive characteristics be recognised.

D _____

Perhaps the most critical element of this view of distance education is the reliance it places on students taking a greater degree of responsibility for their own learning than is generally the case for on-campus study. This expectation sits reasonably comfortably with elements of adult learning theories which encourage respect for students and their experience as well as the familiar patterns of higher degree study.

E _____

It is important to understand that there is a general movement in higher education towards the individualisation of learning generally. Old distinctions between internal and external enrolments will have less meaning over time as the range of resources and strategies in both on-campus and distance teaching are increasingly shared between these modes. While some administrative distinctions will necessarily prevail, the characteristics of good teaching will increasingly be those which allow individual students to pursue their studies in flexible and supportive ways.

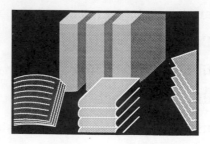

Questions 15–19

In the box below is a list of headings for the 5 paragraphs of Reading Passage 2. Choose the appropriate heading for each paragraph and write the corresponding number **i–vii** in the spaces numbered 15–19 on the answer sheet.
Note that there are more headings than you need.

15. Paragraph **A**

16. Paragraph **B**

17. Paragraph **C**

18. Paragraph **D**

19. Paragraph **E**

List of Headings

i	Anticipated changes in course delivery
ii	Factors influencing the differences between on-campus and distance teaching
iii	Problems experienced by academics
iv	Why support is important
v	How academics adjust to distance teaching
vi	Student responsibility
vii	The main features of teaching at a distance

Questions 20–27

The major characteristics of on-campus and distance learning are listed below, together with those features which are common to both modes. Sort them into their groups and write either **OC** (On-Campus), **DL** (Distance Learning) or **BM** (common to Both Modes) in the spaces numbered 20–27 on the answer sheet. One has been done for you as an example.

Example:	The lecturer does not see the students.
Answer:	**DL**

20. There are opportunities for the exploitation of communications technologies.

21. The lecturer is able to treat the class as a group.

22. Academics may experience difficulty with a different mode of delivery.

23. The teaching methods are familiar.

24. Administrative and support services need to consider students' personal learning needs.

25. Students need to be independent learners.

26. Individual students are encouraged to pursue their studies in the ways which suit them best.

27. There is increasing flexibility in the way students are encouraged to achieve their goals.

You are advised to spend about 20 minutes on **Questions 28–39** which refer to Reading Passage 3 below.

READING PASSAGE 3

ASSOCIATIONS PROVIDE THERAPY FOR SOCIETY

A century and a half ago, Alexis de Tocqueville travelled across the United States to learn more about democracy. One of its underpinnings, he came to believe, was a phenomenon he had not observed in Europe, namely membership by citizens in voluntary social groups.

By the 1950s 'voluntarism', as it came to be known in the US, was being studied diligently by sociologists. Uniquely, Americans continued to increase their participation in organisations such as the parent-teacher associations, league baseball, girl and boy scouts, choral societies, bowling leagues, junior leagues of women voters—the list seemed endless.

Then, in the 1960s, voluntary participation began a steep slide. Robert Putnam, a political scientist, in an ingenious study entitled: *Bowling Alone: Democracy at the End of the Twentieth Century*, began to interpret the implications of the falling figures. Not surprisingly, he forecasts a threat to democracy in the decline of a once vital part of American life.

The reasons for these continuing changes are as numerous as the organisations experiencing them. The rapid movement of women into the workforce is often cited, incorrectly, I believe, as the primary reason for the drop in participation, because they are no longer free to volunteer for community activities or school meetings.

Obviously, it is only one variable. Beginning in the 1970s, real income dropped, which led to the increase in the numbers of people working at more than one job—it now requires two incomes to maintain a similar standard of living that one income provided in 1970. The apparent social isolation has also been abetted by the explosion of new technologies.

Television, tapes, CDs, VCRs and audio-visual cameras have turned the home into an entertainment centre. Another giant leap is occurring through the use of the Internet, the electronic network, that is ultimately likely to be the most revolutionary of all behaviour-modifying technologies.

Putnam's provocative study provides the context within which to consider the implications. No eye-to-eye contact, not even the voice recognition of the phone. Just a depersonalised screen with its written messages on thousands of electronic bulletin boards. Worldwide, the 'community' of Internet users is growing. More than 26 million are already wired in. According to one electronic pioneer, by 2005, if the growth rate continues, every country in the world except Africa will be connected to this global network. It seems unlikely that there will be much time for group activity. Why might this social isolation make a difference? Putnam's figures reveal that being socially connected yields benefits for individuals and society. It is good for your health.

Joining one group cuts your mortality risk in half, two groups are twice as good. If you are part of a social network, someone will notice whether you look well or have been absent from the group. Voluntarism cuts crime. If you know your neighbours' first names it is more of a deterrent to crime than more police. Increasing Parent Teacher Association involvement in schools is more effective than increasing teachers' salaries 10 per cent. Living on a block where people go to church, even if you do not go, means that you will hear about jobs and consequently, will be less likely to be on drugs. Areas with high social connectedness produce better government services, less corruption and more efficiency.

The drop in membership in voluntary associations is marked with a concomitant rise in cynicism and alienation. The convergence of these two growing trends—dropping out and logging on—exacerbates the serious consequences of a drop in political involvement and a rise in social isolation. Life on the Internet is unlikely to lead to the downfall of democracy by itself. Nor is the act of joining groups a guarantee that democracy will thrive. Growth of membership in right-wing religious groups, unbuffered by membership in other voluntary or religious groups, could undermine the very democracy that has thrived on diverse interests.

It is going to require a lot of consciousness-raising to drive home the critical role that social interactions contribute to society, or just as importantly, what their absence could lead to. Even one of the already mythical founders of the electronic revolution, John Perry Barlow, wonders: 'How can you guess what lies in their hearts, when you can't see their eyes?'

Questions 28–30

Complete these statements with not more than **FOUR** words taken from the text. Write your answers in the spaces numbered 28–30 on the answer sheet. One has been done for you as an example.

| *Example:* | 'Voluntarism' may be defined as ... |
| *Answer:* | membership (by citizens in) voluntary social groups. |

28. The drop in voluntary participation has been seen by Robert Putnam as a ...

29. In recent years, because of the drop in real income, more people have had ...

30. Users of Internet have to depend on a ... for information.

Questions 31–35

According to information in Reading Passage 3, match the following kinds of social behaviour with their effects and write the appropriate letter **A–H** in the spaces numbered 31–35 on the answer sheet. The first one has been done for you as an example.

There are more effects listed below than you need.

Example:	Having social links ...
Answer:	**A**

31.   Being a member of more than one group ...

32.   Knowing your neighbours' first names ...

33.   Living near churchgoers ...

34.   Places where social networks are good between people ...

35.   The growth of Internet users ...

List of effects

> **A**   ... helps you stay healthy.
>
> **B**   ... makes it easier to hear about job opportunities.
>
> **C**   ... leads to social alienation.
>
> **D**   ... reduces crime.
>
> **E**   ... produces better schools.
>
> **F**   ... increases your lifespan.
>
> **G**   ... makes drug abuse more likely.
>
> **H**   ... have lower levels of corruption and higher levels of efficiency.

Questions 36–39

Which of the following are mentioned in the passage as being a threat to democracy? Write **YES** or **NO** in spaces numbered 36–39 on the answer sheet.

36.   joining religious groups

37.   joining fundamentalist right-wing religious groups

38.   being part of the electronic revolution

39.   using the Internet

READING TEST 8

QUESTIONS 1–14

*You are advised to spend about 20 minutes on **Questions 1–14** which refer to Reading Passage 1 below.*

READING PASSAGE 1

> ## SUSTAINABLE PRODUCTION

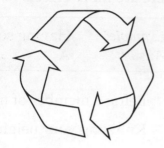

Sitting on my desk are two ball-point pens. One seems unremarkable, just another white, disposable, plastic pen. The second is more curious. It's a small rolled tube of brown cardboard which pulls apart into a body and a lid; only the protruding plastic and brass of the writing tip gives its nature away. It looks like something you might expect to find in a kit of stylish recycled paper envelopes and stationery. But it is planned for more ubiquitous usage to meet the purchasing requirements of many government bodies and companies in Europe; requirements which are increasingly based on environmental criteria.

This cardboard pen is (supposedly) recyclable; the black plastic parts of the pen are from already recycled material (from a shampoo bottle, or a disposable razor, or possibly even another pen). It is a small example of a new trend to design products that can be disassembled and recycled. Pull it apart and the body and lid can be dropped into the paper recycling bin.

The white pen is a manufacturer's demonstration, a prototype. Produced for a European plastics convention, it illustrates another approach to the production of an environmentally acceptable product. The silky feel and the flexibility of the plastic suggests that this is no ordinary stationer's item; so does the embossed 'green' and 'biodegradable' stamp on the barrel. It is made from a plastic derived entirely from corn, manufactured in Italy under the trade name Mater-Bi. If you are prone to chewing the end of your pen, you would find this one quite edible, perhaps even nutritious. Mater-Bi dissolves in water and the manufacturers claim that it leaves only harmless biodegradable organic compounds. After removing the cartridge this pen can go back to fertilize the crops whence it came.

These are just two examples of the transformation taking place in almost all areas of product design; a tantalising glimpse of a sustainable future composed of objects which will be familiar, yet radically different, having evolved, like species, to adapt to new environmental conditions. Consumer products, small disposable items, cleaning agents, domestic appliances, white goods, TVs, computers and cars, clothes and packaging, are all being redesigned to reduce their environmental impact. There is some superficial greening, just the latest ploy from the advertising and marketing division. Many of the more reputable green products, however, represent very large investment in research and design, and in new materials and technology.

These developments are so potentially significant in the light of global environmental problems that government research and development programs in many countries now have new categories of 'eco-design', 'design for the environment' and 'life-cycle analysis'. Recently, Scientific American included 'environmental design' in its list of the 12 critical new challenges for research in the coming years:

'Design for the environment seeks to stir engineers to think about the environmental implications of a product and of its manufacture during the earliest phases of design. These considerations may embrace a sweeping collection of issues: the environmental distress caused by obtaining the raw materials, the toxicity of using and discarding chemicals during production, the likelihood that the production itself can be refurbished, reused or recycled once the consumer has decided to abandon it'.

Questions 1–5

Below are listed some individual characteristics of the white and brown pens together with some characteristics which are common to both. Indicate which is which by writing **B** for 'brown pen', **W** for 'white pen' and **C** for 'common to both' in the spaces numbered 1–5 on the answer sheet.

1.   dissolves in water

2.   can be easily recycled

3.   feels smooth

4.   tastes good

5.   doesn't look like a pen

Questions 6 –11

Complete the following statements using not more than **THREE WORDS FROM THE TEXT.** Write your answers in the spaces numbered 6–11 on the answer sheet.

6.   Many consumer items are being redesigned to minimize their ...

7.   The advertising industry is taking advantage of the ecological trend, sometimes resorting to ...

8.   The more reliable products are the result of financial support for ...

9.   Among the new categories which feature in research and development programs in many countries are ...

10. *Scientific American* believes that ... must be a priority for researchers in the near future.

11. Engineers need to consider carefully ...

Questions 12–14

Questions 12–14 describe the phases in the life of a product. Below is a list of the issues to be considered during each phase. Match an appropriate issue with each phase. Write your answer **A–E** in the spaces numbered 12–14 on the answer sheet. **There are more issues than you will need.**

12. obtaining the necessary raw materials

13. manufacturing the product

14. abandoning of product by consumer

List of issues

A	using dangerous chemicals
B	causing harm to the environment
C	polluting the air
D	possibility of recycling the object
E	making factories safer

READING PASSAGE 2

SEARCHING THE SKIES

From a giant antenna set among the undulating sheep paddocks of rural Australia, one of the great voyages of discovery has begun—the Search for Extraterrestrial Intelligence, or SETI. What the international Project Phoenix uncovers is likely to be so utterly different from our kind, so vastly more sophisticated, as to defy imagining.

The SETI institute, a Californian research foundation, managed to raise $A16 million to fund Project Phoenix, which is using the Australia Telescope at Parkes in New South Wales for its search. To make its discovery, the telescope needs an extra-special hearing aid, a device which resembles an old-fashioned ear-trumpet. Chilled to minus 260°C and crammed with electronics, this feed-horn is the most sensitive built. Responsibility for its construction fell to the Commonwealth Scientific and Industrial Research Organisation radio-engineer Dr Kel Wellington, another true believer since childhood in the existence of intelligence somewhere in the cosmos.

Project Phoenix is a methodical search. Of the 40,000 million stars in our galaxy of similar age and character to our sun, 1000 have been selected which lie within 120 light years of Earth. On a galactic scale, that is a bit like searching a one-metre circle of grass on a 100 metre football oval.

The Parkes antenna zeroes on each star in turn, checking the 200 visible only from the southern hemisphere. The feedhorn listens in on radio channels between 1700 and 3000 megahertz, the most efficient communication frequencies. It is here that the awesome power of modern technology comes into play: the computers scan each of 28 million channels in blocks of 10, searching among the clutter for the elusive pattern of a carrier signal that underlies all complex radio or TV transmissions.

The search's prospects of success are founded on a formula known as the Drake equation, developed by SETI Institute founder Dr Frank Drake. This says that the number of civilizations in the Milky Way galaxy whose radio emissions are detectable depends on:

- The rate of formation of life-supporting stars
- The proportion of those stars with planets
- The number of earthlike planets per solar system
- The fraction of those on which life develops
- The fraction of those where intelligence develops
- The fraction of those where technology develops, and
- The lifetimes over which such civilizations can release detectable signals into space.

To eliminate the dozens of interference events which occur daily, the new search uses something called a FUDD—a follow-up detection device. There is one at Parkes itself and another on a CSIRO antenna at Mopra, 200 km away. If a promising signal is detected by the main antenna it is cross-checked on the FUDDs. If they fail to see it, then it is probably local radio interference—perhaps a farmer on his mobile phone. If they all see it, loud and clear, the excitement begins.

At that point, says Dr Bobbie Vaile, astrophysicist at University of Western Sydney, Macarthur, the first step is to check, recheck and check again. If the signal is still there and is consistent over time the next step is to call up colleagues on radiotelescopes around the world and ask them to home in on the same star and frequency. If they see it too, and the signal is narrow and unnatural-looking, it could come from another civilization.

At this point, she says, the Australian Prime Minister and the US President would be notified and a public press conference convened. 'It certainly won't be kept quiet. It will be a discovery for all humanity.'

And it will be a decision for humanity whether or not to respond. The Project Phoenix team will only listen and learn—they will not transmit any replies. In any event, Vaile points out, even to exchange messages would take many years, maybe lifetimes—and we have been sending radio messages out into the cosmos for nearly a century. A visit on either side is virtually out of the question: to send a ship to the closest star, Alpha Centauri, four-and-a-half light years distant, would consume energy equal to humanity's total use for 20 years.

Question 15

According to the passage which **ONE** of the following statements is true? Write the appropriate letter in the space numbered 15 on the answer sheet.

    A The search for extraterrestrial intelligence depends on an old-fashioned listening device.

    B Dr Kel Wellington designed the Australia Telescope.

    C The stars selected for scrutiny fall within a specified age limit.

Questions 16–18

Choose the appropriate function from the list below for each piece of equipment. Write the appropriate letter corresponding to the function in the spaces numbered 16–18 on the answer sheet.
Note that there are more functions than you will need.

Equipment

16. antenna

17. feed-horn

18. computer

Functions

    A searches for stars within 120 light years of Earth

    B scans channels

    C looks for the clearest signal

    D closely examines 200 stars one by one

    E scans blocks of stars

Which of the following factors are mentioned as part of the Drake equation? Write **Y** for those which are mentioned or **N** for those which are not mentioned. Write your answers in the spaces numbered 19–23 on the answer sheet. An example has been done for you.

Example:	how many life-supporting stars have planets
Answer:	**Y**

19. how life-supporting stars are formed

20. how frequently life-supporting stars are formed

21. how many earthlike planets each solar system has

22. how large the stars are

23. how great the populations of earthlike planets are

Questions 24–30

Below is a list of the steps which would be taken on discovery of an interesting signal. Put them in the appropriate order by writing the letter for each step **A–G** in the spaces numbered 24–30 on the answer sheet.

List of steps

A call press conference
B ask colleagues around the world to check
C check three times over
D decide whether to respond
E call up colleagues in other parts of the world
F contact US and Australian Government leaders
G cross-check through FUDDs

*You are advised to spend about 20 minutes on **Questions 31–41** which refer to Reading Passage 3 below.*

READING PASSAGE 3

THE PROBLEMS OF MATURE JOB HUNTERS

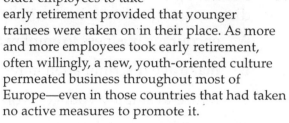

By the year 2000 nearly half the workforce will be over 40 and yet throughout Europe there is a deep ambivalence—if not outright suspicion—towards the capabilities of older workers.

Those over the age of 40 generally take longer to find new employment, but European governments have done little to protect their employment rights. Only Germany, with incentives to business to encourage the employment of older people, and France, with the introduction of legislation making it illegal to use age barriers in recruitment—or to make employees redundant because of their age—have done anything substantive to combat age discrimination.

Yet even in these two countries, there has been no noticeable improvement in the lot of the older worker; indeed in France job advertisements flout the law openly by asking for applicants of a certain age. So, should France and Germany be tightening up their laws and should the rest of Europe follow suit?

Bill Robbins, a careers consultant with outplacement specialist DBM, believes not. He said: 'Legislation against age discrimination has been in existence for well over ten years in the US and Canada, but has had no effect *per se*.

Employers will always be able to find some reason for turning down an older applicant without appearing to break the law. Age laws merely act as a symbol of a commitment to change societal attitudes, and it is these that must be changed if we are to make progress.'

Ironically, it was governments which played a leading role in hardening business culture against older workers in the first place. In the late 1970s many European countries were extremely concerned about the levels of youth unemployment, and France, Germany and

Belgium even initiated incentive schemes for business to encourage older employees to take early retirement provided that younger trainees were taken on in their place. As more and more employees took early retirement, often willingly, a new, youth-oriented culture permeated business throughout most of Europe—even in those countries that had taken no active measures to promote it.

Demographic trends mean that governments are now anxious to slow down the policy of early retirement as they realise that they simply do not have the funds to meet their pension promises. But reversing business attitudes is no easy matter. Dianah Worman, a policy adviser for the Institute of Personnel and Development, said: 'There is a widely held belief that older people are less adaptable and trainable. This is just not true: research has shown that differences in capability are as wide within age groups as they are between them'.

So what can older job-seekers do? On a practical level it is often recommended that applicants either omit their age from a CV or leave it to the end, to ensure that at least it gets read. Yet Tony Milne, an independent careers consultant, believes that the way forward is for older people themselves to adopt a positive attitude to their age when applying for work. 'You can't expect someone else to give you a job if you think you might be too old for it. Many older applicants are extremely aggressive or defensive about their age in interviews. They are immediately labelled by potential employers as difficult characters who would have problems fitting into a new organisation and it is for these reasons rather than their age that they are rejected. If older workers can learn to become relaxed and confident about their age, then I am sure that a change in business attitudes will follow.'

Questions 31-33

Answer the following questions by writing the appropriate letter **A–D** in spaces numbered 31–33 on the answer sheet.

31. Which of the following words best characterises the European attitude to older workers?

    A disapproval

    B dismay

    C distrust

    D dislike

32. France, US and Canada have all taken which of the following steps to discourage age discrimination?

    A encourage business to employ older people by offering rewards

    B make age discrimination in respect of employment illegal

    C refuse to employ younger workers

    D enforce age discrimination laws strictly

33. What did governments do to discourage the employment of older workers in the 1970s?

    A offer early retirement to all employees

    B offer incentives to businesses to take on younger employees

    C only employ young trainees

    D set specific age limits for employment

Questions 34-41

Which of the following points are mentioned in the passage as causing problems for older workers? Indicate by writing **Y** for Yes or **N** for No in the spaces numbered 34–41 on the answer sheet.

34. lack of protection offered by European governments

35. advertisements specifying a desired age for applicants

36. government concern over youth unemployment

37. government refusal to acknowledge the worth of older workers

38. popular beliefs and attitudes favouring younger workers

39. unwillingness of older people to adapt to new methods

40. research into different skill levels in different age groups

41. being negative about their age in interviews

READING TEST 9

QUESTIONS 1–14

You are advised to spend about 20 minutes on **Questions 1–14** which refer to Reading Passage 1 below.

READING PASSAGE 1

A different taste of things to come

The French are turning their noses up at wine and rejecting their croissant in favour of breakfast cereal, the English are turning from tea to mineral water and the Spanish are turning to pizza at an alarming rate. In short, we are beginning to see the evolution of the Euro consumer. That seems to be the message from research conducted by Europanel, an association of research companies across 23 countries which monitor buying patterns using consumer panels.

Social and demographic factors and the marketing strategies of multinational food and drink companies are combining to make the lifestyles of different European nations more alike. The main demographic factors leading to this increasing uniformity across the continent are falling birth rates and easier divorce, according to one member of Europanel. He said: 'The result is smaller households, which rely more on things such as microwaves and convenience foods, whatever the nationality.'

Even the French, who are proud of their cuisine, are turning to the microwave. Latest Europanel figures show that 38% of French kitchens house a microwave, just under the figure of 40% in western Germany. In Britain, the figure is 57%.

The French are also becoming 'less French' as they continue to shy away from wine. Wine consumption in France fell by an average of 6% a year between 1986 and 1992. By contrast, the British are drinking more.

A key demographic factor is average household size, measured by the number of adult residents. Already the spread between nations is quite narrow. Western Germany has the lowest figure in western Europe at 2.2 adults, and Spain the highest at 3.2, followed by Italy at 2.8. The gap will narrow still further because, surprisingly enough, the birth rates in Catholic countries such as Spain and Italy are falling.

Another factor is the rise of the one-person household, frequently misinterpreted to mean harbouring an unmarried or divorced man or woman living alone. Statistically, one-person households include single-parent households, the numbers of which are shooting up. The phenomenon is growing. Forty per cent of Swedish homes are now one-person households, compared with 29% ten years earlier. In western Germany the figure is 35% (30% ten years ago), in the Netherlands 29% (16%), and in Ireland 21% (17%).

In Spain, the one-adult household was so rare a decade ago it did not register statistically; now the figure is 10%. Hence the growth in demand for convenience foods. In Spain, the annual growth rate for pizza sales between 1986 and 1992 was 34% while growth last year slowed a little to 16%. Other factors affect consumer habits. For instance, Piper says that the wider prevalence of central heating in chilly Britain is the chief cause of the decline in the popularity not just of tea, but of all hot drinks. Another major factor is aggressive multinational marketing. After all, the French cannot indulge a craving for sliced bread if all that is on offer is a baguette. The products have to be on the supermarket shelves. In fact, there have to be supermarket shelves. There must be enough space to put new choices on offer.

Once a major manufacturer has won a dominant share in a mature market, it will look abroad for pastures new. Breakfast cereals are one such product. With growth opportunities in the mature British market slowing, manufacturers crossed the Channel.

As a result, cereal sales in France grew by 18% a year between 1986 and 1992, and continued to grow by 10% last year. Similarly, tomato ketchup sales have boomed in such unlikely places as Spain and France, with growth rates of 28% and 18% respectively.

How far the process will go is anybody's guess. Increased choice is all very well, but the prospect of every kitchen in Europe serving up milk-sodden cereal in the morning and microwaved pizza in the evening is surely a depressing one.

Questions 1–4

Complete the following statements with not more than **FOUR WORDS TAKEN FROM THE TEXT.** Write your answers in the spaces numbered 1–4 on the answer sheet. An example has been done for you.

Example:	The association responsible for the research in this passage is known as ...
Answer:	**Europanel**

The eating habits of some European nations are becoming less diverse because of two groups of factors, namely,

1. .... and

2. ...

3. Until recently, it was wrongly believed that the one-person household consisted of ...

4. As soon as it has become successful in an established market, a large company ...

Below are listed some of the lifestyle changes affecting various European nations. Match each change with the country in which it is said to occur by writing the appropriate letter **A–F** in the spaces numbered 5–9 on the answer sheet. One has been done for you as an example.
There are more countries than you need but you may use some countries more than once.

Example :	eating more pizza
Answer:	**A**

5.   eating more cereals

6.   drinking less wine

7.   using more central heating

8.   drinking less tea

9.   having fewer children

List of Countries

A Spain	**B** Italy	**C** France
D Germany	**E** Britain	**F** Sweden

Questions 10–14

Which of the following changes are the result of smaller households according to the reading passage? Write **Y** for Yes or **N** for No in the spaces numbered 10–14 on the answer sheet.

10.   increased use of microwaves

11.   increasing popularity of breakfast cereals

12.   decrease in popularity of hot drinks

13.   increased demand for convenience foods

14.   growth in sales of tomato ketchup

*You are advised to spend about 20 minutes on **Questions 15–27** which refer to Reading Passage 2 below.*

READING PASSAGE 2

Fire Tests

Most fires start in a building's contents, not its structure. Understanding how fire grows indoors—in enclosed spaces—is the first step in limiting its potential for death and destruction. Fire tests have been around for years, and most building codes make reference to them. Some, however, are obsolete, in the sense that they can't accommodate a growing number of new materials in new configurations. Nor can they rank items in order of flammability. What is needed are graded tests that attach numbers to the degree of flammability. These numbers could then be plugged into suitable computer models. The computer could work out the total flammability of an item, depending on what it's made of, how it's put together, and where it's placed.

Computer models are becoming important in fire research. Scientists are hoping that one day, with enough data and sufficiently powerful computers, they will be able to calculate, without actually setting fire to anything, the way a fire will spread in any given building.

A fire indoors is a very different animal from one outdoors. When you put a match to your incinerator, the flames build up steadily. Most of the heat is lost to the atmosphere, so you have no trouble staying close by.

Inside a room, it obeys different and more complex physics, and the danger quietly multiplies. First, instead of a match, imagine a cigarette dropped into the back of a lounge chair. Cigarettes, you should know, are among the major causes of fires in houses. A carelessly discarded cigarette can stay alight in a concealed crevice for as long as 45 minutes. Then, after smouldering away, the chair's upholstery suddenly ignites. Within perhaps 30 seconds, smoke, combustion gases, and heat begin curling upwards, and before 1 minute has passed, they have started building up in a trapped layer under the ceiling.

As the chair continues to burn the layer gets hotter and thicker, and after 2 minutes it starts radiating heat back down to the chair and other furniture in the room. After 3 minutes or so the trapped heat can become so intense that we see 'flash-over'—everything in the room, including combustible gases, has reached ignition point and bursts into flame.

Experiments have shown that some polyurethane armchairs can, 5 minutes after ignition, give out 1-2 megawatts of heat. That's no more than a lively incinerator produces; but when it's confined in a room it can easily induce flash-over. After flash-over anybody still in the room would be dead. People rarely appreciate how quickly a small fire indoors can turn into a deadly inferno. They waste time going to the laundry to get a bucket of water instead of making sure everybody else is out of the house. By the time they get back, the fire will almost certainly be out of control. Billowing clouds of smoke and toxic gases quickly spill through doorways and along halls, enveloping and incapacitating sleeping occupants in the rest of the house.

You can appreciate that modelling the entire course of an indoor fire on a computer is a daunting task. The program needs to consider the flaming combustion zone, the rising thermal plume above it, the hot gas layer beneath the ceiling, and ventilation. Turbulence of air is very difficult to model because large eddies can grow from features as small as 0.1 mm across.

Nevertheless, fire researchers overseas have simplified models to study aspects of fire behaviour in homes, hospitals, aircraft, tunnels, stadiums, shopping malls and airports. For example, the Fire Research Station in Britain has spent 7 years developing 'Jasmine', which can show how air circulates into a burning building and how the smoke layer deepens with time.

In the United States, the National Bureau of Standards has developed ASET, which calculates 'available safe egress time'. This fire-growth model requires figures for rates of mass loss, smoke release, production of toxic gases, and heat build-up. Most existing tests, as we have noted, fail to provide the necessary data. They will need to be modified, or a whole new generation of tests devised.

Questions 15–18

Decide whether the following statements are true or false according to the reading passage and write **T** for true or **F** for false in the spaces numbered 15–18 on the answer sheet.

15. Some older fire tests only show how a fire starts in a building's structure.

16. A computer would be able to grade the flammability of an item.

17. Flash-over can best be prevented with a bucket of water.

18. An adequate computer program for predicting the effects of a fire is not easy to set up.

Questions 19–25

Below is a list of the stages in the build-up of an indoor fire caused by a cigarette dropped down the back of an upholstered chair. Decide where each stage fits in the following table according to the time when it occurs and write the appropriate letters **A–H** in the spaces numbered 19–25 on the answer sheet.

Stage 1	Stage 2	Stage 3	Stage 4
Up to 45 mins. before ignition	Up to 1 min. after ignition	2 mins.	3 mins and after
Example: **A**	19. ———	22. ———	24. ———
	20. ———	23. ———	
	21. ———		25. ———

List of stages

> **A** The cigarette smoulders unseen
>
> **B** The heat trapped in the room intensifies
>
> **C** Smoke, gases and heat rise towards the ceiling
>
> **D** The hot layer beneath the ceiling spreads heat back to the chair and other furniture in the room
>
> **E** A layer of heat is formed under the ceiling
>
> **F** Smoke and gases spread into other parts of the house, endangering anyone who may be there
>
> **G** Everything in the room reaches ignition point and bursts into flame
>
> **H** The upholstery catches fire

Questions 26-27

What are two models for observing fire behaviour that have been developed overseas? Write the answers in the spaces numbered 26–27 on the answer sheet.

26. _____

27. _____

*You are advised to spend about 20 minutes on **Questions 28–42** which refer to Reading Passage 3 below.*

READING PASSAGE 3

SOME MISCONCEPTIONS ABOUT ABORIGINAL AUSTRALIA

When airline pilot Percy Trezise began to explore the rock art galleries of Cape York peninsula in the early 1960s—a hobby that was to obsess him for the next 30 years—the consensus of academic opinion was that Australia had been peopled for less than 10,000 years. Stone tools found in Kakadu have now been dated to at least 50,000 years, and camp sites as diverse as lake Mungo in the Willandra lakes region of NSW and WA's upper Swan River have yielded tools charcoal radiocarbon-dated to between 38,000 and 45,000 years. More than a dozen other sites date to more than 30,000 years—indisputable evidence, says archaeologist Josephine Flood, of the great antiquity of Aboriginal culture.

Thirty years ago, the first Australians were still thought of as a backward race. Trezise recalls in his book *Dream Road*, that there was much sage discussion on whether they were even capable of abstract thought. Since then, reawakened interest in and growing knowledge of Australia's Aboriginal heritage has demonstrated that this is a complex, subtle and rich culture.

The closer we look at Australian prehistory, the more it continues to confound our assumptions. Until recently, the authoritative view was that the population of Australia at the time of the arrival of Europeans in 1788 was probably somewhere between 250,000 and 500,000. But the discovery, beginning two years ago, of a vast Aboriginal graveyard at Lake

Victoria near the confluence of the Murray and Darling rivers has thrown even this into doubt. At least 10,000 skeletons are buried in the sands of Lake Victoria, possibly as many as 40,000. Researchers are wondering if they have stumbled on the demographic hub of an infinitely more populous prehistoric Australia than was ever previously supposed, at the crossroads of two of its greatest river highways. Archaeologist Dr Colin Pardoe of the SA museum says the idea of 300,000 or so people in Australia before white settlement must be radically re-evaluated. 'I believe that we should be thinking 10 times that', he told science writer Julian Cribb recently. As Cribb noted, this would be a greater population than pre-Roman Britain's.

Though Aborigines might see themselves as indigenous (in the sense, as Josephine Flood explains, that they have no race history not associated with this continent) there is no doubt that they were in fact Australia's first migrants. Their springboard was provided by the last ice age, or Pleistocene period, which lasted between two million and 10,000 years ago. So much water was locked up on land that the ocean level dropped perhaps 150 m. There was never a complete land bridge to south-east Asia, but Arnhem Land was linked to Papua New Guinea for most of the past 100,000 years, says Flood, and this would have been one of the easiest routes for ice-age immigrants moving south. What is certain, says Flood in her excellent book *The Riches Of Ancient Australia*, is that once here, the first Australians spread rapidly. The inland would have been dry, but considerably more hospitable than it is today. The inland salt pans were then fresh-water lakes teeming with fish, and the country was much greener.

Questions 28–37

Below is a summary of Reading Passage 3. Complete the summary by choosing **ONE** suitable word from the list below. Write your answers in the spaces numbered 28–37 on the answer sheet.
Note that there are more words than you need.

SUMMARY

Recent 28. _____ findings in Australia indicate that previous ideas about Aboriginal 29. _____ may need to be revised. Charcoal radio-carbon dating of 30. _____ found in different campsites provides evidence of a society that goes back as far as 50,000 years. Furthermore, vast numbers of 31. _____ have been discovered buried in the Lake Victoria region, leading researchers to reconsider their estimates of 32. _____ before white settlement. It appears that there may have been 10 times as many 33. _____ as was previously thought.

If we go back far enough, we can consider the Aborigines as the first migrants because they would have been able to come 34. _____ from Papua New Guinea during the last Ice Age. During this 35. _____ there was a land 36. _____ between Arnhem Land and Papua New Guinea which would have facilitated movement. The land itself would have been more 37. _____ than nowadays with fresh-water fish in the lakes and plenty of vegetation.

List of words

period	civilization	habitable
population	skeletons	inhabitants
link	archaeological	across
century	exploration	out
settled	implements	

Questions 38-42

The table below sets out information from the passage in three categories: former beliefs about Aboriginal Australia, recent changes to these beliefs, and the evidence for these changes. Sort the items of information below the table into their appropriate categories. Write the letters **A–E** next to the numbers 38–42 on the answer sheet.

Table

Former beliefs	Recent changes	Evidence for changes
human beings had inhabited Australia for less than 10,000 years	38. _____	39. _____
40. _____	41. _____	42. _____

Items of information

> A the population was between 250,000 and 500,000
>
> B graves were discovered at Lake Victoria
>
> C the population could have been about 3,000,000
>
> D tools from different campsites were radio-carbon dated
>
> E Australia's Aboriginal civilization goes back about 45,000 years

Reflections on the Reading Test

1. Did you finish the test in 60 minutes?
    ❏ Yes ❏ No

2. Did you look at the questions before you read the passages?
    ❏ Yes ❏ No

    Look at Hints for the Reading Test on page 10.

3. When you couldn't understand a section or weren't able to answer a question did you go on to the next one?
    ❏ Yes ❏ No

    Look at Hints for the Reading Test on page 10.

4. Did you spend a lot of time trying to understand unknown words?
    ❏ Yes ❏ No

    Ask a teacher how to practise strategies for understanding ideas without knowing all the words.

5. Did you answer the questions according to the instructions?
    ❏ Yes ❏ No

    Go back to the test and read the instructions carefully.

6. Were some kinds of questions difficult for you?
    ❏ Yes ❏ No

    If you can, ask a teacher for practice materials with the difficult kinds of questions.

7. Were some reading passages difficult for you?
    ❏ Yes ❏ No

    Practise reading different styles of written English, for example newspaper articles or reports. Try to develop a wider vocabulary.

WRITING PRACTICE TESTS

There are 9 writing practice tests

Time allowed for each test: 60 minutes

<u>**Before you start**</u>
There are two tasks for each test.
For each task photocopy a writing test answer sheet on the next page.
Write your answers on the answer sheet.
You should spend 20 minutes on Task 1 and 40 minutes on Task 2.
When you have finished each test, look at the Model Answers on pages 133–134 and at the Self-Rating Guides on pages 135–136.

WRITING ANSWER SHEET

Photocopy this page to write your answers to each Writing task you practise.

WRITING TEST 1

WRITING TASK 1

You should spend about 20 minutes on this task.

Below is a table which shows the causes of injury by age and their percentage contribution to total deaths during a 12 month period in Australia. Some of these injuries may be termed accidental and some may not.

Describe the information in the table.

Write at least 150 words.

Injury cause	Age category				
	0-14	15-39	40-64	65+	Total
Motor vehicle	40%	45%	29%	21%	34%
Poisonings	1%	4%	2%	2%	2%
Falls	3%	2%	6%	42%	11%
Drownings	19%	3%	4%	2%	5%
Suffocation/Asphyxiation	14%	1%	3%	2%	2%
Suicide	-	26%	31%	17%	27%
Homicide and violence	5%	5%	4%	1%	4%
All other causes	16%	12%	20%	13%	14%

WRITING TASK 2

You should spend about 40 minutes on this task.

Prepare a written argument for a well-educated reader on the following topic:

Human beings do not need to eat meat in order to maintain good health because they can get all their food needs from meatless products and meatless substitutes. A vegetarian diet is as healthy as a diet containing meat. Argue for or against the opinion above.

You should use your own ideas, knowledge and experience and support your arguments with examples and relevant evidence.

You should write at least 250 words.

WRITING TEST 2

WRITING TASK 1

You should spend about 20 minutes on this task.

The graph below shows different population growth rates in some of the world's major cities. Between 1975 and the year 2000, some of these cities are shown to experience changes in population, both within individual cities and in comparison with other cities. Look at the graph and report on these differences.

Write at least 150 words.

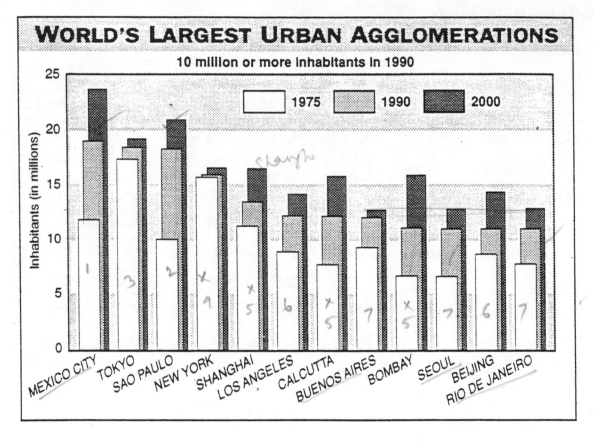

WRITING TASK 2

You should spend about 40 minutes on this task.

Present a written argument or case to an educated non-specialist audience on the following topic:

The best way to reduce the number of traffic accidents is to make all young drivers complete a safe driving education course before being licensed to drive.

You should use your own ideas, knowledge and experience and support your arguments with examples and relevant evidence.

You should write at least 250 words.

WRITING TEST 3

WRITING TASK 1

You should spend about 20 minutes on this task.

The diagram below shows a domestic 'composting' waste disposal unit. Describe the construction of the unit and how it works.

Write at least 150 words.

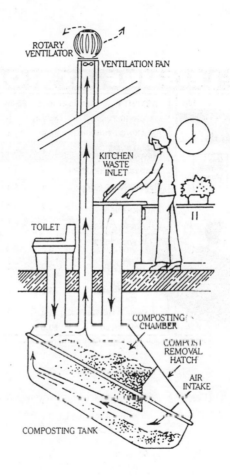

WRITING TASK 2

You should spend about 40 minutes on this task.

Prepare a written argument for a well-educated reader on the following topic:

Forests are the lungs of the earth. Destruction of the world's forests amounts to death of the world we currently know. To what extent do you agree or disagree?

You should use your own ideas, knowledge and experience and support your argument with examples and relevant evidence.

You should write at least 250 words.

WRITING TEST 4

WRITING TASK 1

You should spend about 20 minutes on this task.

The following 2 tables present information taken from a survey into how Australians spend their leisure time at home. By selecting data from the tables, describe the trends as they are shown.

Write at least 150 words.

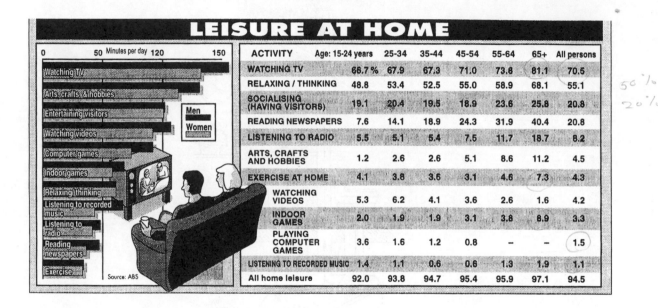

ACTIVITY	Age: 15-24 years	25-34	35-44	45-54	55-64	65+	All persons
WATCHING TV	66.7%	67.9	67.3	71.0	73.8	81.1	70.5
RELAXING / THINKING	48.8	53.4	52.5	55.0	58.9	68.1	55.1
SOCIALISING (HAVING VISITORS)	19.1	20.4	19.5	18.9	23.6	25.8	20.8
READING NEWSPAPERS	7.6	14.1	18.9	24.3	31.9	40.4	20.8
LISTENING TO RADIO	5.5	5.1	5.4	7.5	11.7	18.7	8.2
ARTS, CRAFTS AND HOBBIES	1.2	2.6	2.6	5.1	8.6	11.2	4.5
EXERCISE AT HOME	4.1	3.8	3.6	3.1	4.6	7.3	4.3
WATCHING VIDEOS	5.3	6.2	4.1	3.6	2.6	1.6	4.2
INDOOR GAMES	2.0	1.9	1.9	3.1	3.8	8.9	3.3
PLAYING COMPUTER GAMES	3.6	1.6	1.2	0.8	–	–	1.5
LISTENING TO RECORDED MUSIC	1.4	1.1	0.6	0.6	1.3	1.9	1.1
All home leisure	92.0	93.8	94.7	95.4	95.9	97.1	94.5

WRITING TASK 2

You should spend about 40 minutes on this task.

Prepare a written argument for a well-educated reader on the following topic:

Many lives are in danger when hastily erected buildings collapse because safety standards have been sacrificed to hopes of a quick profit. To prevent disasters of this kind, governments should play a greater role in setting and enforcing safety standards for building construction.

You should use your own ideas, knowledge and experience and support your arguments with examples and relevant evidence.

You should write at least 250 words

WRITING TEST 5

WRITING TASK 1

You should spend about 20 minutes on this task.

The figure below compares the amount of work time required to buy certain products. Comment on these various products and describe the differences for the years 1983 and 1993.

Write at least 150 words.

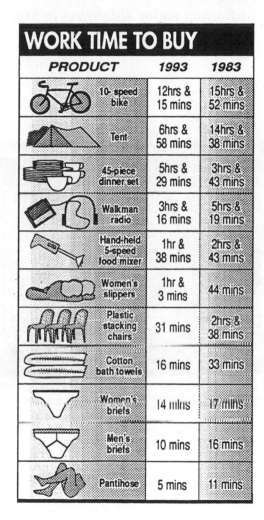

PRODUCT	1993	1983
10-speed bike	12hrs & 15 mins	15hrs & 52 mins
Tent	6hrs & 58 mins	14hrs & 38 mins
45-piece dinner set	5hrs & 29 mins	3hrs & 43 mins
Walkman radio	3hrs & 16 mins	5hrs & 19 mins
Hand-held 5-speed food mixer	1hr & 38 mins	2hrs & 43 mins
Women's slippers	1hr & 3 mins	44 mins
Plastic stacking chairs	31 mins	2hrs & 38 mins
Cotton bath towels	16 mins	33 mins
Women's briefs	14 mins	17 mins
Men's briefs	10 mins	16 mins
Pantihose	5 mins	11 mins

WRITING TASK 2

You should spend about 40 minutes on this task.

Prepare a written argument for a well-educated reader on the following topic:

Children learn best by observing the behaviour of adults and copying it.
To what extent do you agree or disagree with this statement?

You should use your own ideas, knowledge and experience and support your argument with examples and relevant evidence.

You should write at least 250 words.

WRITING TEST 6

WRITING TASK 1

You should spend about 20 minutes on this task.

In all, the world spends an estimated $US25 billion annually, on civilian space applications.

Write a report for a university lecturer describing the trends in the graph below and suggesting reasons for any major differences in expenditure.

Write at least 150 words.

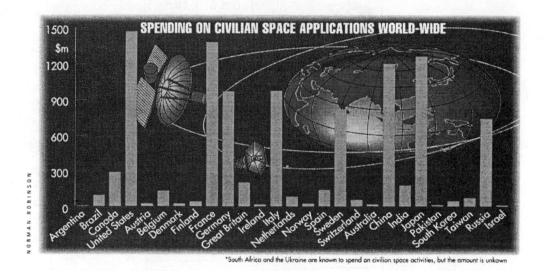

WRITING TASK 2

You should spend about 40 minutes on this task.

Prepare a written argument for a well-educated reader on the following topic:

Zoos are sometimes seen as necessary but poor alternatives to a natural environment. Discuss some of the arguments for and/or against keeping animals in zoos.

You should use your own ideas, knowledge and experience and support your argument with examples and relevant evidence.

You should write at least 250 words.

WRITING TEST 7

WRITING TASK 1

You should spend about 20 minutes on this task.

The graph below shows the rise in the number of one adult households in various European countries between 1981 and 1991.

Write a report for a university lecturer describing the information shown below.

Write at least 150 words.

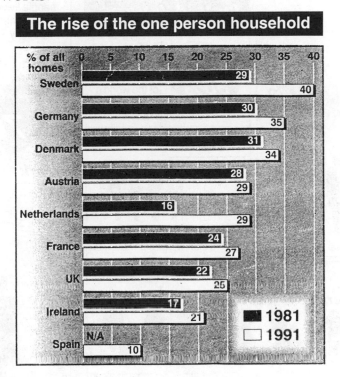

The rise of the one person household

% of all homes

Country	1981	1991
Sweden	29	40
Germany	30	35
Denmark	31	34
Austria	28	29
Netherlands	16	29
France	24	27
UK	22	25
Ireland	17	21
Spain	N/A	10

WRITING TASK 2

You should spend about 40 minutes on this task.

Present a written argument or case to an educated non-specialist audience on the following topic:

Education is recognised as vital to the future of any society in today's world. Governments throughout the world should make education compulsory for all children between the ages of 5 and 15.

To what extent do you agree with this statement?

You should use your own ideas, knowledge and experience and support your arguments with examples and relevant evidence.

You should write at least 250 words.

WRITING TEST 8

WRITING TASK 1

You should spend about 20 minutes on this task.

The 5 figures below give information about women worldwide. Using information from the figures, write a report which describes the status of women in the world today.

Write at least 150 words.

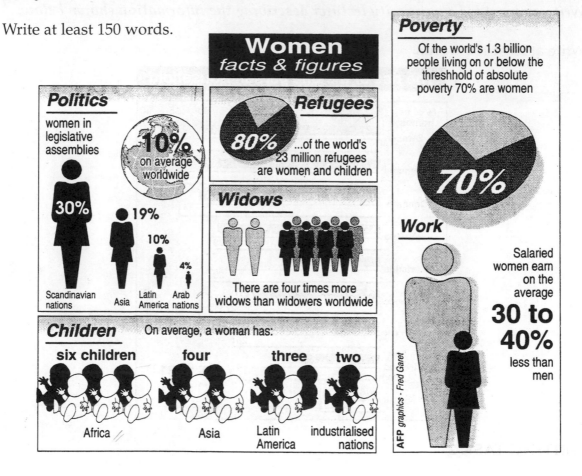

WRITING TASK 2

You should spend about 40 minutes on this task.

Present a written argument or case to an educated non-specialist audience on the following topic:

Tourism is becoming increasingly important as a source of revenue to many countries but its disadvantages should not be overlooked.

You should use your own ideas, knowledge and experience and support your arguments with examples and relevant evidence.

You should write at least 250 words.

WRITING TEST 9

WRITING TASK 1

You should spend about 20 minutes on this task.

The table and the illustration below give some information on sports injuries which lead to emergency hospital treatment. Write a report about the information given.

Write at least 150 words.

Sports Injuries - Nationwide

Sports commonly leading to emergency department treatment in those aged 15 or older:

Sport	Number of injuries	Proportion of sports injuries (%)	Proportion admitted to hospital (%)	Proportion of injuries during competition or practice (%)
Australian Football	10,122	24.5	7.5	83.3
Soccer	3777	9.2	7.1	84.1
Rugby	3636	8.8	10.9	95.0 ✓
Cricket	3408	8.3	5.4	82.8
Basketball	3228	7.8	4.1	82.5
Netball	3098	7.5	2.5	94.8
Hockey	1219	3.0	3.2	95.4 ✓
Martial Arts	882	2.1	5.6	70.6
Squash	787	1.9	6.4	90.9
Volleyball	776	1.9	2.2	79.4

13%

13%

21%

11%

37%

Percentage of injury to parts of the body for all sports

WRITING TASK 2

You should spend about 40 minutes on this task.

Write a balanced essay for an educated non-specialist audience on the topic below:

Technology is making communication easier in today's world, but at the expense of personal contact as many people choose to work at home in front of a computer screen. What dangers are there for a society which depends on computer screens rather than face-to-face contact for its main means of communication ?

You should use your own ideas, knowledge and experience and support your arguments with examples and relevant evidence.

You should write at least 250 words.

Reflections on the Writing Test

1. Were you pleased with your answer to Writing Task 1?
    ❑ Yes ❑ No

2. Were you pleased with your answer to Writing Task 2?
    ❑ Yes ❑ No

3. If you answered 'No' to either questions 1 or 2, were the following some
    of your problems?

    I didn't have enough time.
    ❑ Yes ❑ No

    I had limited knowledge about the topic.
    ❑ Yes ❑ No

    I couldn't interpret the diagram in Task 1.
    ❑ Yes ❑ No

    I didn't check one (or both) of the writing tasks.
    ❑ Yes ❑ No

    I wasn't sure how to answer the question.
    ❑ Yes ❑ No

    Are there any other problems not listed here? Note them down.

    _____

    _____

    _____

    _____

4. If you answered yes to any of the questions in 3, write down a few reasons
    why you think you had problems and discuss these with a   teacher, if you
    can. Think about how you could do better when you take the real test.

5. If possible, ask a teacher for help with some additional IELTS writing
    practice.

    Try to do some writing practice every day.

Model Answers for Writing Tasks

WRITING TASK 1

Test 6

> *In all, the world spends an estimated $US25 billion annually, on civilian space applications.*
>
> *Write a report for a university lecturer describing the trends in the graph below and suggesting reasons for any major differences in expenditure.*

[1]According to the graph, there is considerable variation in spending on civilian space programs around the world. Argentina, for example, spends virtually nothing while, at the opposite end of the scale, the United States spends $1500m. The next highest spenders[2] are France, Japan and China spending $1400m, $1300m and $1200m respectively. Middle range spenders include Germany, Italy, Sweden and Russia, spending in the $700–$1000m range. Among the lowest spenders are Ireland, Australia, Pakistan and Israel spending under $100m. The remaining countries spend between $100 and $300m.

Overall, the trends in the table show the wealthy, developed countries as being foremost in space application spending, while countries classed as developing, or those with very small populations, spend the least. There are some exceptions, like China, which is developing fast and has obviously made space technology a priority. Thus the main reasons for the differences may include wealth, size, political and economic stability and the chosen priorities of each country. (159 words)

Notes
[1]. First paragraph describes 'trends' as asked without needing to give details of each country's spending.
[2]. The word 'spenders' is a good choice to express meaning concisely.

General Comments
Introductory sentence does not waste words by repeating the question.
Answers both parts of the question.
Information is clearly presented and easy to follow.
Sentences are accurately constructed and nicely varied.
Good coherence overall; cohesion achieved through well chosen connecting expressions.

TASK 2

Test 8

> Present a written argument or case to an educated non-specialist audience on the following topic:
>
> *Tourism is becoming increasingly important as a source of revenue to many countries but its disadvantages should not be overlooked.*
>
> You should use your own ideas, knowledge and experience and support your arguments with examples and relevant evidence.

Faster planes and cheaper flights are making it easier than ever before for people to travel.[1] In most 'developed' societies, visiting exotic places is a sought-after status symbol. The tourism industries of both developed and developing countries have recognised this fact and are learning to take advantage of it.[2]

[5] There are, however, some problems associated with this new industry. Firstly[3], there is the increasing crime rate. Some locals see tourists as easy prey because, not only are they in unfamiliar territory and therefore less able to take care of themselves, but also they carry visible items of wealth, such as cameras and jewellery which can be disposed of quickly for a profit.[4]

[5] Another major problem is health. With greater mobility comes greater danger of spreading contagious diseases around the world.[4] One carrier returning home could easily start an epidemic before their illness was diagnosed. Moreover [6] the emergence of many more diseases which resist antibiotics is causing scientists to be increasingly concerned about this issue.

[5] Also to be considered is the natural environment, which can be seriously threatened by too many visitors. Australia's Great Barrier Reef, for example, is in danger of being destroyed by tourists and there are plans to restrict visitors to some of the more delicate coral cays.[7]

These are just three of the reasons why any country should be wary of committing itself to an extensive tourism development program.[8] (232 words)

Notes
[1] Introduction doesn't repeat question.
[2] Tackles question.
[3] Indicates that a number of points will be discussed in order.
[4] Clarifies problem—keeps to the point.
[5] New paragraph for new topic.
[6] Appropriate use of connectors.
[7] Gives examples.
[8] Conclusion rounds off well without repeating question or wasting words.

Self-Rating Guide for Writing Tasks

TASK 1

Answer the questions listed under **A**, **B** and **C**. If you answer 'yes' to most questions, put a score on each line towards **HIGH**. If you answer 'no' to most questions, put a score on each line towards **LOW**. Join the scores together to make a triangle. If your triangle is very small you are weak in at least one area of writing. If your triangle is very big then your overall rating should be quite good.

B

- Have I written accurate grammatical sentences?
- Is my grammar varied?
- Is my spelling accurate?
- Is my vocabulary varied and appropriate?

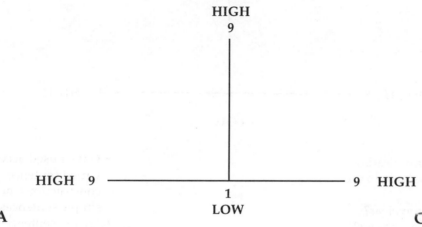

HIGH 9   **9 HIGH**

1
LOW

A

- Have I done what the question asked me to do?
- Is my text clear?
- Is my information well organised?
- Have I used paragraphs appropriately?

C

- Are the sentences in my text well connected?
- Have I used appropriate connecting expressions? (e.g. However, Firstly etc.)
- Do the sentences follow on from each other smoothly, so that they feel connected and the text reads well?

Examples of self-rating

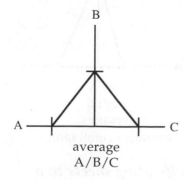

average
A/B/C

average overall rating

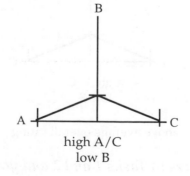

high A/C
low B

above average overall rating

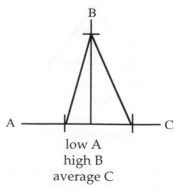

low A
high B
average C

average overall rating

135

TASK 2

Do the same self-rating exercise for Task 2. Note that the rating questions under **A**, **B** and **C** are differerent from those for Task 1.

B

- Have I presented some good ideas and points of view which are relevant to the essay task?
- Are my points of view clear?
- Have I given examples to support my points?

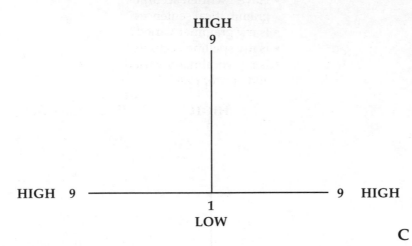

HIGH
9

HIGH   9 ———————————————— **9   HIGH**

1
LOW

A

- Is my text communicating its content effectively to the reader?
- Is the information clear?
- Is the text well organised?
- Have I used paragraphs effectively?

C

- Have I used accurate and varied sentence constructions, not just simple sentences?
- Are my sentences linked by appropriate joining words (e.g. Consequently, After that, However)?
- Have I used a good range of appropriate vocabulary, spelt accurately?

Examples of self-rating

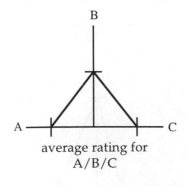

average rating for
A/B/C

average overall rating

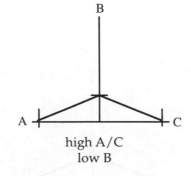

high A/C
low B

above average overall rating

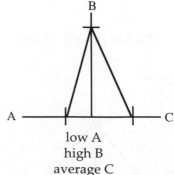

low A
high B
average C

average overall rating

If you can, show your answers to Tasks 1 and 2 and your self-rating sheets to a teacher for comment. Work on your areas of weakness.

136

SPEAKING TESTS

There are 2 recorded speaking tests.

<u>Before you start</u>
Listen to each phase in each test and carry out the tasks on the following pages.
Check the table of Speaking Test Band Scores on page 157.
If you can, practice Phase 3 interviews with a partner using the task cards on page 158.

The IELTS speaking test has 5 **Phases.**

In **Phase 1** the interviewer and the candidate greet each other and make sure they both feel comfortable. The interview will probably be recorded.

In **Phase 2** the interviewer will ask you, the candidate, to talk about your family or your country or something which is familiar to you.

In **Phase 3,** you must ask the questions. The interviewer will ask you to pretend you are in a particular situation where you need to find some information. To get the information you need, you will have to ask the interviewer certain questions, using a card to guide you.

Phase 4 is where you will be expected to talk freely and in a more extended way about your future plans. You will have the opportunity to give opinions or to evaluate specific situations related to your field of study or to your personal interests.

Finally, in **Phase 5,** the interviewer will bring the interview to a close.

Recorded Speaking Test 1

The first interview is with Maria who is a student from Malaysia. She's 18 and is about to enter an Australian university to study Medicine. Here are a few details about Maria.

PERSONAL DETAILS

Family name: MAHAMOOD

Other names: MARIA

Nationality: MALAYSIA   First language: MALAY LANGUAGE

Occupation: STUDENT

Work experience: AS A STUDENT

How did you learn English? AT SCHOOL

What are your personal interests? TRAVELLING, WATCHING TV READING NOVELS

What are your future plans? TO BECOME A DOCTOR

Why are you taking this test? I WANT TO GAIN EXPERIENCE

Maria

Phase 1

A

i) Before listening to Phase 1 of the interview look at questions 1–7 below. Guess Maria's responses to these 7 questions and write your guesses on a separate sheet.

Questions 1–7

1. Hello Maria. Could I have a look at your personal details?

   My guess _____ *Maria's response* _____

2. Right now, and you come from Malaysia?

   My guess _____ *Maria's response* _____

3. What part do you come from?

   My guess _____ *Maria's response* _____

4. Is it very sunny?

   My guess _____ *Maria's response* _____

5. Do you um do you have any brothers or sisters?

   My guess _____ *Maria's response* _____

6. Right and are you the eldest?

   My guess _____ *Maria's response* _____

7. And are some of them studying in Australia as well?

   My guess _____ *Maria's response* _____

ii) Listen to Phase 1 and note down Maria's responses. Stop the tape at the end of Phase 1. Are your responses similar to hers?

In your opinion, were Maria's responses:

    a too long?   **b** about right?   **c** too short?

Circle either **a**, **b** or **c**.

If you circled **a**, which responses could Maria have shortened?

_____

_____

If you circled **c**, what other things could she have said?

_____

_____

Discuss your opinions with a partner if you can.

B

If you can, work with a partner. Ask and respond to similar questions about your own country and family. If you are working alone, write down your questions and record your responses on a cassette recorder.

Phase 2

A

i) In Phase 2 Maria is discussing her studies. Read questions 8–22 quickly. Which of these topics is mentioned? Tick (✓) the box if the topic is mentioned.

a) medicine as a field of study	
b) hospitals	
c) illness	
d) department stores	
e) emergency	
f) medicine as a career	

ii) Read the questions again. Circle the questions to which it is **not** possible to answer just 'yes' or 'no'.

Questions 8–22

8.   And er it says here you're hoping to get into Medicine at university?

9.   Um tell me a little bit about what happens when you're ill in Malaysia? What happens when somebody's sick at home?

10.   Do you have er general practitioners, doctors who come to visit homes?

11.   And er what sort of um illnesses are common in Malaysia—what do people often complain about—being sick, being off work?

12.   And are the colds that you get in Malaysia similar to the colds you get in Australia?

13.   Tell me a little bit about the nearest hospital to Terangannu.

14.   Is it a big hospital?

15.   What sort of departments does it have?

16. And er what do you do in Malaysia when you want an ambulance? Do you have a special number you can ring?

17. When, when did you first start to get interested in er Medicine as a field of study?

18. Was there someone in your family who encouraged you, or was it just your own idea?

19. Right er is she er involved in Medicine in some way?

20. So what er what appealed to you about Medicine as a career?

21. Glamour?

22. But it's certainly an er an occupation that's well respected in Malaysia?

B

i) Listen to Phase 2 of the interview. As you listen, try to note down Maria's responses to each question.

ii) Rewind the tape and listen to Phase 2 again. Choose one or two questions which, in your opinion, Maria responds to well, and one or two questions to which she responds not so well

Write the question numbers down and give reasons for your choices in the box below.

Question number	Responded well (**W**) or not so well (**NW**)	Reasons

Compare numbers and reasons with a partner if you can.

C

Using questions 8–12 as a guide, write down 5 questions about your area of study. Find a partner to ask you these questions. If you are working alone, write down each question and record your responses onto a cassette recorder.

Phase 3.

In the next phase of the speaking test, Maria is going to ask the questions. The interviewer will tell her about a certain situation. Maria needs to find out some information about it. She will need to ask as many questions as she can in order to get as much information as possible. The interviewer will give her a card which explains the situation and which has a few suggestions for questions on it. She may take a few moments to look at the card before she starts asking the questions.

A

Before you listen to the tape, first look at Maria's card and decide what questions you would ask in this situation. Write a few questions down. Try not to use the exact words written on the card.

Maria's card looks like this.

Task   **WEEKEND CAMP FOR NEW STUDENTS**

There is a weekend camp being organised for new students.
Find out:

- the purpose of the camp
- where it is being held
- arrangements for getting there and back
- the cost

My questions:

- _____

- _____

- _____

- _____

B

Read the interviewer's responses to Maria's questions, numbered 23–31. Which of your own questions would fit the interviewer's responses?

Interviewer's responses 23–31

23. Yes, well we decided to er to have these camps some years ago because we think it's a good way for students to get to know each other in an informal way before their courses start so er it's a sort of getting to know you type camp.

24. Er the camp is at a beach about 50 kilometres away from the University. It's sort of south of the University, along the coast.

25. Yeah yeah near a seaside.

26. Well er there'll be a bus which will pick up er students from the University and return people to the same spot at the end of the camp so there's no problem with transport.

27. Yeah well it's a comfortable bus, a University bus.

28. I think so.

29. I'm afraid there is a cost yeah though it's not too bad. It's $65 for the whole er stay and that includes all meals and all transport so er it's on a long weekend Friday till Monday and er all meals are included so that's that's very cheap.

30. So are you interested in going?

31. I hope you do.

C

Listen to Phase 3. Write down Maria's questions and compare them with the ones you wrote.

Maria's questions:

- _____
- _____
- _____
- _____
- _____

Do you think any of her questions are poorly constructed or follow the words on the card too closely? Which ones? Rewrite the ones you want to change.

Phase 4

In this phase Maria is being asked further questions about her career plans.

A
Look at questions 32–45. How are these questions different from those in Phase 2? Choose the expressions which you think best describe the differences.

- longer
- more demanding
- more varied
- asking for more opinions

- more specialised
- simpler
- more interesting

Discuss your choices with a partner if you can.

Questions 32–45

OK. Let's er let's get back to thinking a little bit about er your future er we know that you want to er to study Medicine but er

32. **have you any thoughts about what sort of Medicine you're going to specialise in at the end of your studies?**

33. Do you agree with that?

34. What sort of pressure do you imagine er er it would involve?

35. Yeah well I was going to say that er er in some ways one could argue that maybe it's er more suited to er a woman than a man? Many women are midwives in other countries.

36. Do you have midwives in Malaysia?

37. And and do they deliver many of the babies? Or is it mainly doctors in hospitals?

38. Right. Is there any any reason for that particularly?

39. So they don't have a long training?

40. So do you agree with that view? Do you think er doctors do know more about ...?

41. It's difficult to generalise, isn't it?

42. So do you think there's a a big need for er doctors who are specialists in infant care or delivering babies in Malaysia? Is is that a growing area of need?

43. Is there a fast growing population in Malaysia?

44. So it could be a very important area for your country if you choose that?

45. Well, perhaps at the end of your studies you'll be more confident because you'll have learnt so much more? Is that a possibility?

B

Listen to Phase 4 of the interview. Circle 'yes' **Y** or ' no' **N** below.

Compared to Phase 2:

does Maria develop her answers more?	Y	N
does she use a wider vocabulary?	Y	N
does she express more opinions?	Y	N
are her answers more interesting?	Y	N
is she speaking more confidently?	Y	N

C

Look back at Question **32.** How would you respond to it for your field of study? What other questions could be asked about your country in this section? Think about your country and your life in five years' time.
Write about five questions on these topics. If you can, practise with another student. Have a conversation about each other's country and field of study. If possible, record yourselves.

Phase 5

This is the final phase of the interview.

A

Below are the interviewer's concluding remarks. What could Maria say here in response to the interviewer? Write down some possible responses.

46. Well, er I'd like to thank you Maria for er taking part in the interview and I wish you the best of luck with your studies.

---

47. It was nice to talk to you.

B

Now listen to Phase 5. Are Maria's responses friendly? Does the interview end in a relaxed or in a formal way? Which is more appropriate in your view?

Assessing Maria's Band Score

The assessment for the Speaking tests is made on a scale from 1–9.

> | The candidate can't say very much in English | | The candidate uses English like a native speaker |
> | --- | --- | --- |
> | | 1 — 2 — 3 — 4 — 5 — 6 — 7 — 8 — 9 | |

Using this scale, circle a number to show what you think Maria's score would be.

If you can, find another student who has done the same exercise and compare your ratings of Maria's interview. Discuss your reasons for the score you gave.

Interviewer's comments.

Read what the interviewer says about Maria. Were your impressions similar to those of the interviewer?

Maria would probably just gain a ✍ in the speaking test. She had no difficulty understanding all sorts of questions and in the final stage she was able to use more extensive vocabulary and develop some areas of questioning reasonably well. She was generally fluent in her use of the language; there were no long pauses or laboured constructions of sentences. In Phase 3 she was able to converse more formally and ask questions with reasonable ease. Maria's weaknesses were caused primarily by her youth and her lack of experience and knowledge. She was unable to develop some responses because of lack of knowledge, for example, of the hospital system in Malaysia. Her pronunciation was sometimes a little unclear particularly her stress patterns and she had one or two areas of grammatical error which are typical of the Malaysian variety of English. The interviewer asked a lot of questions to keep her contributing to the conversation, but natural shyness kept many of her responses short. The shortness of Maria's responses was mirrored in the tendency of the interviewer to ask short questions.

Recorded Speaking Test 2

The second interview is with Pehr. Pehr is 25 years old and is from Sweden. He's a marketing manager who is in Australia for three months studying English. Here are some details about Pehr.

PERSONAL DETAILS

Family name: *Abrahamsson*

Other names: *Pehr*

Nationality: *Swedish*   First language: *Swedish*

Occupation: *Student*

Work experience: *Bartender, Marketing Manager*

How did you learn English? *Primary school and high school*

What are your personal interests? *Downhill skiing, windsurfing and golf*

What are your future plans? *English for the moment*

Why are you taking this test? *Who knows, interesting*

Pehr

Phases 1 and 2

A

In the first two phases Pehr is being asked questions. Before you listen to the interview, read Pehr's responses to the interviewer. Predict what the interviewer's questions were about, for responses **1, 2, 3, 4, 5, 10, 12, 15**, and **17** below. Write your predictions on a separate sheet.

<u>Pehr's Responses to Phases 1 and 2</u>

1. **I'm fine, thank you.**
2. **Yeah. That's right. From Europe, from Sweden. Yes.**
3. **Well, I've been study since I was er 10 years old maybe, partly in the primary and later on in the secondary school in Sweden, yes.**
4. **This is my first trick trip to Australia. Yes, it is.**
5. **Well I haven't been in other places in Australia but later on I think I will go to other cities, yes.**
6. Well, I'm for the Christmas later on I'm invited to Brisbane. To the Gold Coast as well, so I think I will pop up there for a while.
7. Very humid and very warm. Yes, that's right yes.
8. I think I can stay inside and if I go out I have to go to the beach, instead I'll take a bath, take a swim.
9. Yes, I do. I think I would do that later on when I come to Europe this winter.

<u>Your predictions.</u>

Question 1

_____

_____

Question 2

_____

_____

Question 3

_____

_____

Question 4

_____

_____

Question 5

_____

_____

10. **Some particularly... memorable occasions? Yeah, last year in fact I was there just before the Olympic Games when I was visiting the Val d'Isère slopes. Very nice area. Scary slopes. Somewhere it's built very steep.**

11. Well, they're very steep and icy. Of course that's exciting as well at the same time.

12. **No not really. I just hurt my tum (*thumb*) some years ago. That can create a lot of problems because you use your hands and arms a lot when you ski. So ...**

13. Yes. Right.

14. Yeah. I've seen a a a woman once for a couple of years ago who broked her leg and you could see her bone sticking out from the flesh. It's quite ... yes ... it's not so funny.

15. **Yeah. Yes you have to be careful and not do stupid things. Yes, that's right.**

16. Perhaps in Australia. Yes that's right. But I think it's very important to have something to do during the summer and something to do at winter, during the winter.

17. **Yes for 6 years I was competing er before and I'm looking forward because in a couple of days I will go down to Victor Harbor further down for some wind surfing I hope.**

18. Well, I was, it was a er the, in, in just in Sweden National League, how do you put it, in funboard and waveriding, yes.

19. No, I just was average person who just love it for fun.

20. Yes. Yes. Especially with this weather coming now and during the summer, I would like... looking forward to that.

Question 10

_____

_____

Question 12

_____

_____

Question 15

_____

_____

Question 17

_____

_____

B

Listen to Phases 1 and 2 on the tape to see if your questions were similar to the interviewer's questions.

C

Rewind the tape and listen again to Phases 1 and 2 and assess the responses Pehr gives to the interviewer, according to the categories below. For each of the three categories, fluency, grammar and vocabulary, mark X on the line to indicate your assessment. Then, if you would like to, read the transcript on page 173 to reflect on your assessment.

Fluency

not fluent							very fluent
1 — 2 — 3 — 4 — 5 — 6 — 7 — 8 — 9							

Grammar

low accuracy							high accuracy
1 — 2 — 3 — 4 — 5 — 6 — 7 — 8 — 9							

Vocabulary

limited variety							wide variety
1 — 2 — 3 — 4 — 5 — 6 — 7 — 8 — 9							

Phase 3.

In this phase, the candidate asks the questions. The interviewer will tell you about a certain situation. The interviewer will give you a card which explains the situation and has a few ideas for questions on it. You need to find out information about it by asking as many questions as you can. Take a few moments to look at the card before you ask the questions. Try not to use the exact words on the card for every question. The interviewer responds to your questions.

Pehr's card looks like this.

Task **FURNITURE ENQUIRY**

You are new at the university and you have found some cheap accommodation, a one bedroom flat. Unfortunately, the flat is unfurnished.

Ask the Accommodation Officer for assistance with finding inexpensive furniture.

- rent or buy furniture
- new or second hand furniture
- where to find items needed
- where to sell when studies completed
- advice on most useful items

A Think about some questions you would ask the interviewer. Write them down.

- _____
- _____
- _____
- _____
- _____

B

Listen to Phase 3 of this interview. As you listen, circle any expressions in the box which describe Pehr's conversation style and his manner. Add suitable adjectives of your own.

> **direct**
>
> *humorous*
>
> *relaxed*
>
> quiet
>
> friendly
>
> **talkative**
>
> r u d e
>
> nervous
>
> informal
>
> *shy*
>
> _____   _____ (your own)

Compare the questions Pehr asks with the ones you wrote. In what ways are they different?

C

Below are the questions that Pehr asked. Read them through, and compare them with the prompts on the card. Think again about what kinds of questions he asked and whether or not you think he has asked enough.

1.   Well, can you help me please?
2.   Well, it's like that I have found cheap accommodation here in our last day in the newspaper and er it's a one bedroom flat and but it's unfurnished so I want some advice how I could find some cheap furniture because I'm a student and I haven't so much money as you.
3.   Well I think it would be a year, I think, say, yes.
4.   So it's not so big difference between renting or buying from, if I'm here for a year?
5.   OK. So it's possible to... to sell them later on to another student?
6.   Great. Where do you think I can find some cheap used furniture then for a student?
7.   No. Yes. Preferably, yes.

152

8. Yeah. From other students maybe?

9. OK. Here. In Adelaide?

10. OK. Good. And um, what do you think? Is there, is there any possibility to use desks here in er at the university? Or do you think I have to buy a desk as well?

11. If you want to study, yes. Maybe.

12. OK. OK. Thank you very much.

Note: Remember, every candidate approaches the same task in a slightly different way. There is no one fixed list of questions for this Phase 3.

Phases 4 and 5

A

In the final two phases of the interview, Pehr discusses several topics. Listen and tick any topics that Pehr discusses.

Holidays ☐

University ☐

Studies ☐

Unemployment ☐

Recession ☐

Taxation ☐

Trade ☐

United Nations ☐ 👆

B

Rewind the tape to the beginning of Phases 4 and 5. Listen for Pehr's response to the interviewer's question about taxation in Sweden. When talking about taxes, Pehr says to the interviewer 'I don't really agree with you about that...'
What does the interviewer say that causes Pehr to say this?

The transcript of Pehr's responses for Phases 4 and 5 is on the next page if you want to listen and read.

> Note: It is important to recognise that it is appropriate and often refreshing to have IELTS candidates express alternative viewpoints. You are being tested on your ability to express your opinions; you are not being tested on the opinions you hold.

C

Listen again to a later section in Phase 4. Pehr uses the word 'expectations' several times. What do you think he means? Discuss with others or write your thoughts down.

Although it is not easy to pinpoint exactly what Pehr means, he uses fluent and challenging English and the conversation is maintained. Discuss with a partner if you can, how this might affect his final rating.

Transcript of Pehr's responses to Phases 4 and 5

1. Yes. I'm... after my high school, secondary school in... Sweden, I went to the university— University of Lund. It's in the southern part of Sweden in a part called Scania. Quite near Denmark and Germany... and er I studied majorly in Business Administration, Economics and Commercial Law at university for four and a half year.

2. Yeah. That's right. But the, the recession lately, in Europe especially had created a a condition there the most of the movements and the interesting thing is sometimes in the public sector.

3. So therefore maybe there'll be another possibilities there instead cause it's quite downgoing or in the private sector. Yes.

4. Yes in fact when you hear the word Sweden you sometimes connect it with low unemployment figures but in fact today we have had quite high unemployment especially among young people and academic people, yes.

5. Yeah, that's right.

6. Yes, but since 2 or 3 years ago that had been changed not only the income taxation, also for example for taxation on alcohol and things... just to move the country much more towards the EC[1], cos we have, had hand in, a EC enrolment for a couple of years ago... so we intend to be a part of the EC in '95, yes.

7. **Generally. Well as most people as you said hate the word tax. It's not so funny when the tax bill comes. Um, but in fact I will, I'm not really er agree with you about that because I think Sweden have lower taxes now than Australia, in fact. Especially when you if you have in a higher level of wages.**

8. **Well. It's not no, it's not over 50 percent. It had been 80 percent.**

9. Quite often, quite often it's just 35 or 30. Which I think is quite alright.

10. Well OK.

11. Well OK. It depends if you talk about median or average figures it's working pretty good.

12. Yes. I see in in some parts, there of course if you look at these trade areas as the European market... and recently we have heard about the the er agreement in America... and some people in Australia for example don't understand that this will make it a little bit harder for Australian companies to export to these areas in America because there would be a trade war.

13. **But the important thing is not only the facts always, sometimes is it the expectations. So, I see some expectation in the world today, yes even if we have specially in Europe we have some wars there as you know, in the Eastern Europe and that's affect the whole economy but the expectation is much more important than the effects.**

14. **Expectations... if you today if you have seen the statements and comments in the newspaper about this agreement in the... in America you see that most people are quite positive even if they know that it will in some cases hit Australia in a bad way.**

15. NAFTA[2]. Yes. Right. And, but the the dynamic effects are, are forecast or expected to be more important than these smaller effects on special businesses... in Australia and throughout the world. So...

16. Right... long term gains and with it big big communities, like, or big areas with free trade, will create high competition, and then more movement of people and better allocation of resources.

17. We would hope so. Yes.

18. You've hit the recession. One of the first countries who hit the recession and that have been with us a long time. Stucked because you have had other your business partners have hit the recession later on. So you have had been hit a little bit harder than we have had. That's right .

19. Thank you.

---

[1] EC—European Community (Now European Union)

[2] NAFTA—North American Free Trade Agreement

Assessing Pehr's Band Score

Using the same scale (1–9) as you did for rating Maria's interview page 146, rate Pehr's speaking performance by circling a number in the box below.

The candidate can't say very much in English							The candidate uses English like a native speaker

1 — 2 — 3 — 4 — 5 — 6 — 7 — 8 — 9

Now if you can, find another student who has listened to Pehr's interview and compare your ratings just as you did for Maria's interview, and discuss your reasons.

You may now like to read the interviewer's comments on Pehr's performance and check the score she gave him in the answer key. Did the interviewer give Pehr the same score that you did?

Interviewer's comments.

The interviewer gave Pehr a score of 🖐.
It was a lively discussion and the communication was good. Pehr gave quick responses to the questions and was strong on question formation. Instances of use of formal and informal language were appropriate. Pehr's grammar was reasonable, although he had minor inaccuracies. Pehr's vocabulary was almost native-like in terms of variety. Clearly there was a struggle with some responses as Pehr's argument was not always perfectly developed nor expressed logically.

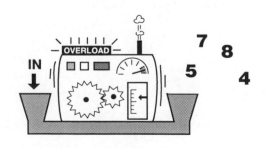

What do the Speaking Band Scores mean?

You have now had the chance to listen to two practice interviews and read the comments which the interviewers made on the two candidates. Think about what kind of speaking abilities justify a rating of 6 or above.

Look at a table of Speaking Test Band Scores* below. Write in some other expressions which might usefully describe and distinguish each level on the band scale.

Score	Description
9	Like a native speaker; _____
8	Very fluent; can use formal and informal language; _____
7	Quite fluent; wide vocabulary; _____
6	Forms questions well; _____
5	Some difficulty asking questions; _____
4	Pronunciation difficulties; limited vocabulary; _____
3	Hesitant; incomplete sentences; _____
2	Extremely limited vocabulary; no sentence structure; _____
1	Not really able to communicate in English at all; _____

Compare your descriptions with a partner if you can.

* Unfortunately, we are unable to give you the official descriptions of the Band Scores because they are confidential.

Find a partner to practise a complete interview with. There are some more Phase 3 task cards on the next page. You might like to record your practice interviews so that you can listen to them again and give yourself a rating.

ENJOY YOURSELF!

Find a partner and practise Phase 3 of the Speaking Test using any of the task cards below.

Task   **SPORTS PRIZE**

The interviewer has just won a sports prize. You would like to know about the prize. Ask as many questions as possible to find out the details.

- sport
- kind of prize
- training practice
- feelings about winning
- plans for the future

Task   **INQUIRING ABOUT A CHEAP HOLIDAY**

You are a new student and you are very interested in seeing some parts of the country. Ask the Student Travel Officer about some cheap holidays. You would like to go away for one or two weeks.

- places to go
- cost
- type of transport
- accommodation
- brochures/information leaflets

Task   **STUDYING AT THE UNIVERSITY**

You would like to enrol in The University as an undergraduate student. Talk to the Student Admission Officer to find out the course details.

- pre-requisites
- length of study
- hours per week of study
- commencement date
- cost per year

TRANSCRIPTIONS

LISTENING TEST 1

Section 1.

Barbara.   Mm. According to the sign, the computer room is around here somewhere. It says room B100. This is B 105. Oh there it is, down at the end of the corridor. Computer room—B100. Easy to find.

B.   Excuse me. Are you in charge here?

Assistant.   Yes. Sort of.

B.   Then perhaps you can help me. I need to use a computer to type an assignment. What do I have to do?

A.   Well, are you a student?

B.   Yes I am. First year.

A.   O.K. Have you used a computer before?

B.   Yes. I've done a fair bit of word processing.

A.   That's good. That'll save you a lot of time. Well, there're 40 computers in this suite and they're all available for student use. Staff are not supposed to use the computers in this room. The computers are in constant demand so you'll need to book well in advance. O.K. now, here's a timetable and booking sheet. It's in that book which is kept just inside the door here. You can reserve a computer for 2 hours at a time. If no-one else has reserved it after that you can continue past your booked time, but you can be sure that won't happen very often. And the computer room is open from 8:00 in the morning to 10:00 at night Mondays to Fridays and on weekends and public holidays from 9:00 to 5:00.

B.   Mm. What do I do if something goes wrong with the computer?

A.   There's usually someone here at least from 9:00 in the morning most days in case something goes wrong. So you'll really only have a problem if you're here before 9.

B.   Well that all seems to be straightforward enough. What about printing? Can I do that here too?

A.   Sure can. There are 4 printers. They're down at the end there. You have to pay for each sheet of paper you use.

B.   Where do I get the paper from?

A.   You can use your resource card for that. I'll show you. Look over here.
You insert the resource card into the printer like this and you can use whatever value you have remaining on the card. It's just the same as photocopying—about 10 cents a page. And you also have to supply your own disk of course.

B.   Do I have to worry about viruses on the disk?

A.   No. Don't worry about that. There's an automatic scanner in each computer to make sure students' disks haven't got viruses. Have you got your student card with you?

B.   Mm. Yes. I think so. Just a moment. Oh, here it is.

A.   O.K. I just need to take down your student number for the records. Let's see. That's number 95102975. O.K. Now you can go ahead and book yourself in. Every time you book a computer you write your name and your student number in the time slot alongside the number of the computer you're going to use.

B.   Thanks. I'll make a booking right now.

A.   O.K. Oh, and one more thing. No eating or drinking in here. The computers are on a diet.

B.   Oh right!

Section 2

Ricardo.   Here we are. Brochures for 1 day excursions. Let's have a look.

Barbara.   Mm. A riverboat trip. That looks interesting.

R.   Yeah. It does. Where does it go? And how do we get to the river?

B.   It says to go by bus to the river. Mm. The bus trip takes about an hour. That costs $5 per person each way. Then the boat goes along the river for 4 hours. And we can get a meal on the boat. That sounds good.

R.   How much does it cost?

B.   Well, the boat trip costs $20 and the meal is extra if we want it. I suppose we could take our own food to save some of the expense. Then the bus picks us up at the other end of the boat trip and brings us back. It sounds great, but it's a bit expensive—$30 each altogether, and that's not counting the food and drinks.

R.   Yes. It would be relaxing but it is a bit expensive and we wouldn't get much exercise sitting on a bus and a boat, would we.

B.   No. You're right. What about horseriding or cycling? Can you ride a horse?

R. Not very well. I've only ridden a horse twice in my life and that was a long time ago. How much does it cost?

B. Let me see. Horse riding's a bit expensive too—$30 for 2 hours. That's to hire the horse and all the equipment you need, including a riding helmet. And we'd have to get to the stables. It looks like it's a long way from here. We'd probably have to go there by bus. And that would be an extra cost.

R. Er, what about cycling? That shouldn't be too expensive. Here we are, er, mountain bikes for hire. $30 a day. But $20 of that is a deposit and you get it back when you return the bike. I wonder how far away the cycle hire place is.

B. I'll ask the assistant. Excuse me. Can you tell us where the cycle hire place is, please? Is it far from here?

A. No. It's not far at all. I'll show you. You go out there to Riverside Drive and turn left down towards the Railway Station. Before you get to the Railway Station, you'll see a small car park. There's a little path which goes down this side of the car park. Go all the way down to the end and the bicycle hire place is on the left. It's the only place there so you can't miss it. It's clearly marked with signs and only 5 minutes' walk from here.

B. That's terrific. Thanks. Well, what do you think? Cycling looks the best, doesn't it? That should give us enough exercise. And we can take our own lunch and have a picnic. Now all we have to do is to decide which direction to cycle in.

R. Great. Let's go. We can talk about that while we're walking to the hire place.

B. Hello. We'd like to rent 2 bicycles for the day. We saw this brochure in the university recreation office. It says that you rent out bikes for $10 a day plus deposit. Is that right?

A. I'm afraid the rate has gone up. That's an old brochure. It's $15 a day now. But still $20 for the deposit. And if you want to hire a set of panniers to carry your things, that's an extra $5. But the bikes are all good. They're checked regularly and well maintained. And there's a helmet and a repair kit with each one. You have to wear a helmet by law.

R. That's right. Is there any limit to how far we can travel?

A. No. The only limit is your own energy. But the bikes do have to be returned before dark as there aren't any lights on them. It gets dark by 6.00 pm so you have to have them back by 5.30.

B. That's OK. Is there anywhere you can recommend as a good place to cycle to?

A. You can either go towards the hills or to the beach if you're energetic. If you're not so energetic, there's a cycling track along the river. A lot of people take that.

R. Well I think this should be a good way to spend the day. We'll hire 2 bikes then. Here's $70. We won't need the panniers. We'll take our back packs.

A. Have you got any identification? A student card or a driver's licence will do.

B. &
R. Yes—I think so.

A. And can you fill in this form with your names and addresses and a contact phone number please? And both sign if you don't mind. Thanks. Here's your receipt. That's for 2 lots of $15 plus 2 deposits of $20 each. You'll get your deposits back when you return the bikes of course. By 5.30 at the latest don't forget.

B. We won't. Thanks. See you later

R. Bye.

Section 3.

Secretary. Good morning. Strings and Brass Imports.

Barbara. Good morning. My name is Barbara Sanchez. I'm a student at the University. I'm doing a Post Graduate Diploma in Business Administration and I need to do 3 weeks' work experience. My lecturer, Ms. Farrow recommended that I contact your company to see if I could do my work experience there. I wonder if I could speak to the personnel manager please. I think his name is Mr. Lewis.

S. Yes. That's right, but unfortunately Mr. Lewis is out of the office at the moment. You can make an appointment through me if you like though.

B. Yes please. I'd like to come for an interview as soon as possible. I'm free all day tomorrow or the next day.

S. Just a moment please. What about 9:00 tomorrow? Or any time between 9:00 and 11:30 if you prefer?

B. No. 9:00 would be fine thanks. I can use the rest of the day to study then.

S. 9:00 in the morning then. Good-bye.

B. Yes. Thank you. Good-bye.

B. Good morning. My name is Barbara Sanchez and I've got an appointment at 9 o'clock with Mr. Lewis.

S. Oh, yes. You phoned yesterday, didn't you? Mr. Lewis is waiting for you. You can go straight through to his office.

B. Thank you.

B. Good morning. I'm Barbara Sanchez.

Mr. Lewis. Good morning. Come in and take a seat. Now, what can I do for you?

B. I'm a student at the university. I'm doing a Business Administration course— a Post Graduate Diploma, and I need to do 3 weeks' work experience as part of my course. My lecturer, Ms. Farrow suggested I contact you as you've allowed students before to do work experience in your company. She thought you might accept me. I've got a letter of reference here from Ms. Farrow if you need it.

Mr. L. Thanks. I'll need that. Yes. Er, this company seems to have a good relationship with the university. We've had quite a lot of students here over the past few years. It seems to work well. We usually take students who are in the er second half of their course. What stage are you at?

B. I'm almost at the halfway mark. I've got some exams to do first in 2 weeks' time. Then I'll be ready to start before the beginning of the second semester. But I thought I'd get this organised before the exams start.

Mr. L. That's a very responsible way of thinking. It's a good idea to get in early. I'm sure there's a lot of students who'll be looking for placements in work experience soon.

B. I could start in 3 weeks' time if you like.

Mr. L. Do you understand what 's involved in this type of work experience?

B. I think so. Ms. Farrow explained the procedures thoroughly to all the students. I have to work regular hours, according to company policy and while I'm here I'll have the opportunity to experience different sections of the company. At the end of the 3 weeks I have to write a comprehensive report on what I've learnt as an assignment for Ms. Farrow and I have to give the Director of the company a copy of it as well. And I understand you send a report about my work to Ms. Farrow and that will also be a part of my assessment.

Mr. L. That's right. You say you'll be able to start in three weeks. Mm. That's the 15th isn't it? Yes. I'll have to discuss this application with the Director of course. And I'm sure you'd like to know as soon as possible if you've been accepted.

B. Yes please. Because if I'm not accepted I'll have to apply somewhere else.

Mr. L. I should be able to let you know by the end of the week. Just give your phone number and address to the secretary before you go. Well, thanks for coming in Ms. Sanchez. We'll be in touch with you by the end of the week. Good-bye.

B. Good-bye Mr. Lewis.. Thank you for seeing me.

S. How was the interview?

B. I hope it was alright. It seemed to go well but it's hard to tell. Mr. L. has asked me to leave my name and address so that he can contact me.

S. Yes. Of course. Your name is Sanchez. That's S–A–N–C–H–E–Z isn't it?

B. Yes. That's right. And first name Barbara. Ms. My address is 17a John Street, Forestville.

S. Joan Street?

B. No John Street. That's right. And the Post Code is 5035. And you'll need my phone number won't you. That's 3320578.

S. 322?

B. No 3320578. Yes. That's it. But I'm usually at the University in the mornings.

S. I'll make a not of that too. Call in the afternoon. Good. We'll be in touch then. See you later.

B. Thanks very much. Goodbye.

Section 4

Interviewer. Well now we come to the most interesting part of the research. Can you tell us exactly who is most in danger and perhaps why?

Researcher. Well, according to the latest findings, it appears that passengers are at greater risk of injury than drivers in road accidents, with the rear left seat being the most dangerous place in a car. The claim is based on research into accident situations involving more than 18 000 victims which found the driver's seat was the safest place to be in crashes involving one or more vehicles.

I. That's quite surprising.

R. Yes. The conclusion was that, contrary to

public perception, seating positions and vehicle types had a greater effect on the severity of injuries than speed and people's ages. These findings have obvious implications for future vehicle design and road safety campaigns. While the wearing of seat belts and speeding have been targeted in education campaigns, other factors also need to be considered. For example, vehicle manufacturers should be taking a closer look at providing more protection for passengers. In this investigation, the researchers used econometric models to identify the probabilities of receiving different levels of injury and how these changed with variations in the attributes of road users. The attributes included sex and age, and where relevant, blood alcohol readings of the victims, the type, make and age of the vehicle and the nature of the collisions. The research also found that females were slightly more at risk of sustaining serious injuries than males, and light trucks were more dangerous than any other type of motor vehicle. As I said, the safest seating position was the driver's seat and the left rear seat was the most dangerous.

I.   I'll have to remember that.

I.   Could you give some idea of level of risk in terms of different accident conditions?

R.   O.K. Well, just as an example of what could happen I'll give you some statistics. A typical victim occupying the left rear seat in a 10 year old car involved in a head on collision at 42 km/h would have a 10–20% chance of requiring treatment at the scene, a 60–70% probability of requiring hospital treatment and a 20% chance of being killed. We can compare this with an almost zero probability of a 33 year old male driver being killed in the same accident, a 70% probability of requiring treatment at the scene and a 30% chance of needing hospital treatment. It also appears that the effects on injury probabilities of a large increase in speed are surprisingly small. When vehicle speed is increased from 42 to 100 km/h, the probability of a person requiring roadside treatment is 60%, that of requiring hospitalisation is 40% and that of being killed is zero. It's possible that these findings may be a reflection of vehicle design, or it may be possible that drivers take defensive action to increase

their own chances of survival and therefore inadvertently decrease the survival chances of their passengers.

I.   Well, thanks very much for sharing those very interesting findings.

That is the end of Listening Test 1.

LISTENING TEST 2
Section 1.

Alex.   Hi, John. I haven't seen you for a long time. What have you been up to?

John.   Good day Alex. Studying. Seems that university life is much more time consuming than I originally thought.

A.   Yes, I agree. I'm really pleased that I finished my studies. All I need now is a good job.

J.   Yeah, the employment situation is not too good. I hope it improves by next year when I'll be looking for a job.

A.   Anyway, let's not get serious. You're probably looking forward to experiencing a bit of city life. You've spent most of this year living in the country.

J.   Yeah, living so far from the city makes it difficult to come here as much as I'd like. Still I guess a four and a half hour round trip is not too bad. That's two hours to get here and two and a half to get back.

A.   Why does it take so long to get back?

J.   Oh. Because the train from the city is a mail train. It stops at a few country towns along the way. But I'm here now. What shall we do? We've got the whole day. My train back home doesn't leave until 10:30 tonight.

A.   Well, I thought you might enjoy having a drive around the city, followed by lunch at Ocean Beach and then we could go to an early evening movie. What do you think?

J.   I've been to Ocean Beach a few times but I wouldn't mind going again. No, come to think of it, I've heard that one of the Navy's latest submarines is visiting Deep Harbour and the public are allowed on board between 10:00 and 4:00 today. How about going there and then having lunch after? There's a cheap seafood cafe close by. We could still have time to see a movie too.

A.   Sounds great. Let's go. My car's parked around the corner.

J.   What sort of car do you drive these days?

A.   Remember the van I bought last year? I got rid of it last month. I've now got a two door sedan. It's nothing special but it takes me where I want to go. By the way, what do you want to see tonight?

J. I don't know. What's on?

A. Um. There are a few good shows on. It depends what you're interested in. What do you feel like watching; science fiction, horror, drama comedy, adventure, martial arts? There's a lot to choose from.

J. I don't mind science fiction. I'm not keen on martial arts. I quite like comedy and drama but adventure's my favourite. Movies with a hero battling against the odds, they're always great. Horror? I've not seen many lately, apart from that latest Dracula movie, which I must say was a bit disappointing. But I usually find them exciting.

A. Well there's a new adventure movie on tonight at the um Circle Cinema. Can't remember the name but it's set in the Amazon jungle. Would that do?

J. Yeah, why not.

A. Before we go, would you mind if we stopped off at the Panorama camera store in Long Street?

J. No worries.

A. Excuse me. I think there's something wrong with my camera's film winding mechanism. I can't seem to put the film on any more.

Assistant. Let's take a look then. Mm. Yeah, I think we'll need to make some adjustments. Um, it looks like we'll need to replace the winding mechanism. But I'm afraid we won't be able to do the job straight away. Would you be able to leave it here for a week? We're very busy at the moment but I'm sure we could repair it in the next few days. Is that satisfactory?

A. Oh. Okay, I guess. But I was hoping to get it done on the spot.

As. Well we normally could manage that but I'll need to order the replacement part from our camera supplier in Newtown. I'm sorry. That's the best I can do.

A. All right then. That'll be okay. Do you need any details?

As. Yeah just a few. What's your name?

A. Alex Ursini. Ursini's my family name.

As. How do you spell that?

A. U–R–S–I–N–I. Alex.

As. And address?

A. 65 Baron Road Howell.

As. 69 Baron Road H.....

A. No. No. It's 65.

As. Oh, sorry. 65 Baron Road Howell.

A. Yep.

As. Postcode?

A. 8590

As. And what's your telephone number at home?

A. I don't have a phone at home but you can always leave a message with my next door neighbour.

As. And what's their number?

A. 9211067

As. Good. I think we've got enough details. Now, the camera will be ready Thursday 1st of February.

A. Sorry. Look. I can't pick it up until the following Tuesday. Tuesday the 6th.

As. Oh, okay, that will be fine. We'll see you Tuesday.

Section 2

Angela. Wow, it's really crowded!

Lani: Yeah. There certainly are a lot of students here today. How many do you think are here?

A. Oh, I couldn't really guess but I suppose it could be close to fifty or sixty.

L. I hope we're not all looking for the same books.

A. With a bit of luck, being the first day of the book sale, we should be able to find at least some of the books on my list.

L. Yeah. There are mountains of books to look through.

A. Oh, I don't think it will be all that difficult. With the two of us here, we stand a good chance.

L. Well, here goes.

A. Great! Guess what I've just found?

L. What?

A. *Wine Science.* It's by Bookman? It's quite cheap considering it's a thick book and in fair condition too. Pity it's the 1983 and not the 1993 edition. But quite good for $4.15.

L. Not a bad start, eh? And we've only just arrived.

A. Some of the books here are a little on the expensive side, aren't they?

L. Yes, but these second hand texts are much cheaper than buying them brand new. Hey. Look what I've got here, *Grapegrowing*. Is it on your list? It's 1993.

A. Fabulous! This is one of the main books in the course and apparently, it's used in second year as well. And it's not really expensive at $30. There's no author though. Um. It's edited instead. By MacLean. The condition is quite good too. Considering it's a classic book in the wine industry, it's pretty good value. I'm glad I brought my backpack along. I think it's going to be very useful with all these books we're finding.

L. Oh look. Here's another one on your list, *Wine Making.* It's by someone called Brown.

A. Let me see. Um. Yes it's on my list. How much is it?

L. It's the fourth edition and I can't read the price. The ink's smudged. $30 I think. No, it's $13.

A. The fourth edition and it's immaculate. What a bargain! This one normally sells for $45 in the university book shop.

L. We are doing well!

A. Yes. I'm so pleased you're helping me Lani.

L. My pleasure. What are friends for? *Red Wines of the World.* Is that on your list? Able's the author.

A. What price has it got on it?

L. $25

A. Mm, it's the latest edition, the second. But doesn't it look dull? Very technical with only a few illustrations. I'm not too excited about it. Still, it looks in fair condition. I suppose I should buy it.

Section 3

Tina. I'm speaking this morning to Terry Greening, City University's Environment and Resources officer. Good morning Terry.

Terry. Hi Tina.

Ti. I understand that our university has recently begun a program for recycling paper. Can you tell us something about it?

Te. Uh, yeah Tina. Well the university has been recycling office grade paper for about three months now. And in fact, it's totally voluntary and we find that most staff agree that there's a lot of need for it and in fact, many people even do some recycling in their own home.

Ti. Mm, I'm sure.

Te. Yes, so we thought it'd be a good idea to introduce it here at the university. Um, initially we began in the university Student Records office where we found there was a lot of office paper waste.

Ti. I can imagine.

Te. Mm. And it was surprising really. The waste came largely from computer print out paper and photocopies and even old examination papers.

Ti. Oh. Right. And how did you come to begin the paper recycling process?

Te. Well er, there's a government collection service that arranges for used office paper to be collected from various locations and then it takes this paper to a recycling plant to be recycled into paper products like um, wrapping paper and envelopes, er paper bags things like that.

Ti. Mm. Right.

Te. And it's called Paper Saver. Er, and they sell large cardboard boxes to people and offices for placing used office paper inside.

Ti. Oh, I think I've seen some of those.

Te. Mm. They're quite good.

Ti. It sounds like a good idea. How much are the boxes?

Te. Oh it's not too bad. They only cost $5 each. And they're quite strong and they're reasonably large. In fact, they can hold up to 20 kilograms of office paper each.

Ti. Mm, that's quite a bit isn't it? So for example in Student Records, how many boxes would you need there?

Te. Um, in Student Records we've got 8 boxes.

Ti. Mm. And how often do the boxes get full?

Te. Well, they fill up about every couple of months or so. And what we do is, we place 4 boxes in various locations and when they're full, we immediately exchange them with another 4 replacement boxes.

Ti. Oh. Right. Turn about.

Te. Yeah, so in fact, we don't have overflowing boxes. Um, we just fill them up as we go along while we're waiting for Paper Saver to pick up our full boxes.

Ti. Oh, I see. That sounds good. And do you think people tend to use the reverse side of paper as well?

Te. Mm, in theory, we'd like to think so.

Ti. Yeah.

Te. But, admittedly yes, that's a slight problem. We encourage people to do this by having 4 separate categories.

Ti. And er, what are those?

Te. Er first, there is reuse paper—paper that is photocopied on one surface only. And secondly, we have recycle paper—paper that has no unused sides at all, then there's scrap paper. Of course that's paper that's ripped or in small pieces, or for some reason it's just not useful. And lastly, there's coloured paper. This includes non-white envelopes and manilla folders.

Ti. It's separate, isn't it?

Te. That one's separate, yeah. And so to answer your question, we encourage staff to dip into the reuse paper box, the one-sided paper, and try and use sheets of paper for things like writing memos, and so forth. What's left over from that, we send to the university library to be used by students for note paper or in whichever way they wish.

Ti. That's good. There are plenty of ways then for people to use paper on two sides and reuse paper. Do you ever find anything undesirable in the boxes?

Te. Occasionally.

Ti. For example?

Te. Well, there have been things like plastic lunch wrap, banana peels and tissues and in fact, once I even heard that someone found a gold watch!

Ti. Oh, that's not so bad. That's good. Good luck.

Te. Mm.

Ti. Was the owner ever found?

Te. She was actually. It didn't take her long to notice her watch was missing.

Ti. Of course. But overall, would you say that paper recycling scheme is working well?

Te. Definitely! Yes, I really think it's a great idea. And in fact, It's a good way of saving our resources, you know, saving trees being chopped down.

Ti. Yes of course. Very important.

Te. The less paper, the fewer trees we need. And er, there seems to be a trend now towards recycling paper.

Ti. Yes, yes. I think so.

Te. Yeah, you can buy envelopes, greeting cards and many other paper products made from recycled paper. And, I think the great thing is that everyone feels they're doing something good when they buy products from recycled paper.

Ti. Of course. I think so. Yes I think most people do share that view. Well thank you Terry for your time this morning. That was very interesting, very informative. And let's hope that people in the university can carry on recycling paper.

Te. Thank you.

Section 4

Vice Chancellor. I'd like to welcome Dr Wright to our series of lectures on 'Excellence in Science'—and I must say, judging by the numbers of you in the audience out there, this is the most popular lecture we have had all year! So rather than take up any more of your time, I'd like to introduce Dr Wright and the topic 'The Commercialisation of Science and Technology.' Dr Wright.

Dr Wright. Thank you. Science and technology and the role of commercialisation in that area, it's an interesting question. It's an issue which is going to be increasingly important, world wide.

Let me just begin by giving you an overview of the relationship between science and technology and research development and innovation. These are terms which people often use as if they mean the same thing. Essentially, science is that which is done to generate new basic knowledge, knowledge in areas where nobody has previously researched. Generally, that's done in the universities and the government funded research centres, of one sort or another. The larger international companies also do some of that, their own research I mean.

Technology is really to do with the application of science. It turns scientific discoveries into a useful product, or a useful service. If I may compare science and technology, I could say that science provides the fundamental knowledge that explains a phenomenon, whereas technology takes that understanding and transforms it into a useful thing. It's very much like a pendulum and a clock. The pendulum is the part of a clock whose movement, back and forth, makes a clock work. The clock is the useful product that has a function of telling the time. Therefore, science can be compared to that swinging motion within the clock and technology is the total object—the clock. That's the sort of difference you're looking at.

Research, development and innovation are aligned, in that research is closely related to basic sciences. Development is the process of taking the basic scientific idea or item and running it through to the development of products and services. Innovation is really about putting that product and service into the market place. So innovation is about the creation of a new set of ideas and products and a new set of ways of delivering them.

Now in terms of commercialisation of

165

technology, the most important thing nowadays is the difficulty that countries have with funding. That is, getting enough money with which to develop scientific ideas into useful products and services. It's very expensive. For every dollar you spend on basic research, it costs a company $10 in development and another $10 in marketing.

Many companies today just cannot afford that. The other thing of course, is for every profitable research idea, there's an average of nine ideas that come to nothing. So, only one out of ten is taken to the final production stage. I'll stop here for any questions.

Terry.   Oh excuse me. Er, I'd like to know what happens to all of those so-called 'unsuccessful' ideas?

Dr W.   Yes it's a continuing problem. Most of them are, of course, lost forever. A few may eventually reach the production stage through the persistent efforts of interested individuals but this requires a great deal of time and finance on the part of the inventor, or owner of the idea. Most people, however, just don't have enough resources to invest in a product that cannot guarantee a profitable return on their investment. No more questions? OK. Now, returning to my last point about companies and research ideas. Many ideas look wonderful on paper but they are often impossible to utilise in an inexpensive enough manner, or, having done so, the product doesn't really work, or it's unacceptable for various reasons. So before too long, the technology becomes outmoded, it becomes old technology—like record players. For example, you don't see companies today investing money in, record players do you? Why bother? I imagine that in the not too distant future, young people won't even know what a record is.

At present, there seems to be a movement in the commercialisation of research and development towards the need for companies, large and small, to subcontract. That is, companies pay other specialised individuals or organisations to do research on their behalf. It's becoming the practical solution. It's only the very large companies who still retain their own research and development units.

So occasionally, there's a situation where a company has to commercialise but can't do it alone. It has to get help. Sometimes, this help may come from a smaller company, or, what's happening more often these days, companies turn to universities and ask them for assistance with the development of new technologies. You find that's a world wide movement. It happens in every country that has a reasonable number of high tech firms. It happens in Europe, the United States, Asia, Australia, wherever. It's important that governments understand the need to continuously research and develop, and governments should be aware of this need for domestic companies to work closely with firms overseas. The reality is on an international scale, if a company wants to be part of an international movement, governments need to encourage and facilitate the interaction of the domestic firm with its overseas counterparts. This doesn't always happen because of the huge costs involved in doing so.

However, it's an exciting period, a very, very exciting period for science and technology.

Now, returning to my point about the need for further research and development it seems to me that today ...

That is the end of Listening Test 2.

LISTENING TEST 3

Section 1

Adam.   Perhaps we can begin now. How many students do you cater for here?

Julie.   There's probably about 100–150 though they don't all use the coffee shop every day

A.   And, er, what hours are you open —9:00 to 5:00 ?

J.   Er, about 9:30 to 4:00.

A.   I see. Do you work on your own here all the time?

J.   Mostly. When I'm busy I sometimes have a bit of extra help.

A.   Mm. And um, do you have a constant stream of students all day or just at lunchtime?

J.   No. I mainly have students coming about 10:30, 11:00 to about 11:30—it can get really crowded then, more so than for lunch—and then again at 12:30 on and offish to about 2:00. Then at 3 o'clock there're a few and then you get others, you know coming and going.

A. This is a very smart eating area—do customers sit down and get waited on or do they queue up?

J. They queue up and ask for what they want. Then they can point to their choice if they don't know the right word.

A. Do you find that overseas students have a sweet tooth like Australians are s'posed to have? Do they buy lots of cake?

J. Yes, they do. They buy a fair bit of cake.

A. Oh, and um do they make requests for particular kinds of food?

J. No, no, not really. They usually like what I've got to offer.

A. And when when you have cake, is there one kind that seems to be more popular than others?

J. Well, I think the chocolate cream cake always seems to be the favourite and then you've got your apple cake and that, which is also popular.

A. Mm. Are there any other differences between staff and students' tastes?

J. I don't know. The staff usually go for the hot lunches, you know, curry or spaghetti and so on but a lot of the students bring their own lunch.

A. Tell me, er, when you're so busy how do you manage to deal with the dirty plates—do you do you collect all the plates off the tables or do you have a trolley, or what?

J. Students are usually quite good about that—they bring their plates—to a designated area—actually that bench over there in the corner against the wall.

A. Oh, I guess that's better than bringing them back to the counter, or leaving them for you!

J. Yes, that would be really messy if they did that!

Policew. Can I help you, sir?

Adam. Well, I hope so. You see, I left my briefcase, with my passport in it, on the bus this morning.

Pw. Right then, I'd better have a few details. What's your full name?

A. Adam George O'Riordan. That's oh I'll spell it. O–apostrophe–R–I–O–R–D–A–N

Pw. And your address?

A. 30, Rose St, Marryatville

Pw. How do you spell Marryatville?

A. M–A–double R–Y–A–T–V–I–double L–E

Pw. And you say you lost your passport. Do you happen to know the number?

A. Yes, luckily I kept a record of it in my

diary. Here it is. It's MY679043

Pw. And what time did the loss occur?

A. Well, I caught the 8:40 bus into the city and it would have been about 10 minutes after I got off the bus, and I'd reached the lecture theatre and was going to get a pen out. You see, I had an armful of folders which wouldn't fit in the briefcase, so I forgot I should 've had it till then. So, the lecture starts at 9:30 and I get off the bus about ten past nine.

Pw. OK. Now can you tell me the number of the bus?

A. Yes, it was the 504. I sometimes catch the 506, but I know I didn't this morning, because the 506 is a bit later and I have to run to get to the lecture on time.

Pw. Fine. Have you reported this to the Transport Authority Lost Property?

A. Yes, yeah, I've done that, but they said I should also come to you in case someone brought it in, particularly as my passport was in it.

Pw. Was there anything else in the briefcase?

A. A couple of library books that I wouldn't really want to lose and some notes, that's about it.

Pw. No money?

A. No, I've got my cash in my pocket.

Policem. Hey, Jill, did I hear you taking down details for a lost passport? Guess what?

Pw. What? Tell us. What's happened?

Pm. You won't believe it but someone just turned in a briefcase containing a passport and they found it on the 504 bus this morning.

Pw. Well, how about that Adam? Looks like you've had a lucky day after all.

Section 2.

Adam. Does your work bring you into contact with many overseas students, Sue?

Sue. Occasionally. As you know, a solicitor's work is to advise people about their rights when they have any problems understanding how the law operates. They may need help because of injury to themselves or their property—if they've been attacked or robbed, for example. But these are not by any means the main problems I deal with.

A. Really? We know more about crime, I suppose, because we read about it in the newspaper or see it on TV. What other things do people come to you, for help with?

167

S. There are lots of things which don't get nearly so much attention. Sometimes it's to do with relationships in the community, as when bills aren't paid or contracted work isn't completed, or neighbours disagree. At other times it's to do with people not understanding the law and their responsibilities and this is probably where overseas students have the most difficulty. One interesting example is customs laws—something which every new arrival has to come up against.

A. What is it that overseas students find most difficult to understand about Australian customs regulations?

S. I think it's a shock to many people arriving here for the first time to find out how many things are prohibited—everyday food items, for example. I mean, when I've been travelling overseas, I've been quite amazed at the lack of concern in some countries about food being brought in from other parts of the world without any check.

A. You mean, people arriving into other countries don't have to declare any foodstuffs at all?

S. In some countries there are lots of warnings about drugs and firearms and there are usually limits on alcohol and tobacco and perhaps perfume, but food's not mentioned.

A. Yes, I suppose I never thought about it till I came here. You can take anything you like into England, as far as food is concerned that is.

S. You see, here, you can't even drive from one state to another with a few apples and oranges for the journey. You have to leave all fruit in a special deposit box at the border. It's the same when you're flying. There are signs to remind you not to bring any fruit into some states, though they don't usually search your bags, unless there's a fruit fly epidemic or something.

A. Hm. With those kinds of regulations between states, it's no wonder that they're so strict about what you can bring in from overseas. Of course, farmers would be wiped out if some pest were introduced which destroyed their whole crop. It's easy to understand why you should take steps to prevent that.

S. And with food being such an important part of many cultures it can be difficult for some people to realize they're not allowed to bring in delicacies from home for friends and relatives here. I'm defending someone at the moment who has exactly that problem.

A. Oh? What happened?

S. It's an interesting case. Have you got time for a cup of coffee? I'll tell you about it if you like.

A. That'd be great!

Section 3

Sue. It was a boy from Vietnam coming to study here and he was caught bringing in some processed pork and some Vietnamese sweets for his relatives.

Adam. Doesn't exactly sound criminal!

S. No, well, he was going to be staying with them and no doubt the family wanted to show their gratitude and appreciation so they decided to send something from home that might not be available over here.

A. Of course! I can imagine doing the same myself.

S. Yes, but the leaflet attached to the customs declaration says very clearly in red letters that no food of any kind may be brought into Australia and every passenger coming in must sign a declaration to say that they're not carrying any food with them.

A. That's right, I can remember doing it, too. So this chap is really in trouble, is he?

S. He certainly is! After he'd told the customs officer that he wasn't carrying any food, the goods were found in his luggage.

A. Oh, so they searched him!

S. They did. And of course he looked really guilty, being caught with that food in his suitcase.

A. He must've been shocked to realize that the customs officer thought he had broken the law and he was being charged with a criminal offence! I mean, most people understand about drugs and weapons and such obviously prohibited items but I suppose they don't see food in quite the same way.

S. The thing is, we are an island and we do have crops and livestock to protect. The average person doesn't understand how dangerous some imported foodstuffs can be.

A. Then it sounds like you're in for a tough time defending this chap. Um, what 're you going to say?

S. You're right. There are problems.

However, there are a couple of things that could be used in his favour. One is his level of English and the other is the question of who packed his case for him.

A. I'm surprised to hear that lack of English could be a defence. I always thought that not knowing the language of the country made no difference in considering whether a person had broken the law or not

S. Of course that's true, but in this case we will be trying to convince the magistrate that this student's inability to understand spoken English was the reason why he couldn't answer the customs officer's questions and we hope that he'll accept this defence.

A. But if he were going to study at University here, wouldn't his English have to be pretty good?

S. Apparently his written English wasn't too bad, but like most new arrivals, he couldn't understand the Australian accent.

A. I see, and what about the other point about packing his luggage himself?

S. Well, of course, it's harder to make someone responsible for the contents of their luggage if they didn't do their own packing and there are a number of reasons why this student may not have packed for himself.

A. Oh? What are they?

S. First of all, he told us he didn't get his visa until after the course had started. This meant he had to get his bags packed in a hurry and his mother helped him. She was most likely responsible for putting in the food items and in the rush she may not have even got round to telling him. The food may have been destined for relatives in Australia but some of it may also have been intended for her son. Remember, he was leaving home for the first time, travelling to a strange country and his mother probably imagined him feeling homesick and wanted to provide some comfort.

A. And she was probably worried about what on earth he would get to eat in a foreign country!

S. Exactly! And this is the evidence I'm using to build up some sort of defence.

A. Good luck! Let me know what happens!

S. O.K. I will.

Section 4

Lecturer.   Although most Australian cities are pretty safe compared with their counterparts in other parts of the world, it is still important to be aware of the safety precautions Australians would never think of omitting. If you are used to a less urbanized lifestyle, there may be some things that are taken for granted here, but which might never have occurred to you.

For example, locking up—an essential part of daily life! If you live in a Hall of Residence, this will not be such a problem. You have only to ensure that your room is locked when you leave—and that you have the key on you. If, however, you share a house or flat, then it's essential to check all the doors and windows before you go out for the day. Statistics show that most burglaries happen during daylight hours, when the occupiers are out. Even if you think your house or flat is securely bolted and barred, don't leave a lot of money inside. The safest place for your cash is the bank. Take out only enough for your immediate needs and in that way you will avoid disaster.

Furthermore, don't flourish large wads of notes in public to impress your friends—not everyone watching may be a friend, and while we're on the subject, keep valuables–passport, jewellery under lock and key. Better to be safe than sorry! During the day, at school or college, never leave your handbag or wallet unattended, on a desk or in the library or classroom, say. Most institutions will warn you about this and although you may think your fellow students are very honest people, there are always individuals you don't know about in public places who may not be able to resist temptation. Likewise, always lock your car or bicycle and never leave any valuables where they can be seen by passers-by.

Another important area where advice is often needed has to do with going out alone at night. Even in a comparatively safe city like Adelaide, there are places where locals do not go unaccompanied at night. They do not go into open parkland areas, for example, where lighting is minimal and shadows deep. Nor do they go down narrow streets or dark alleys. The most important rule here is to use commonsense. Don't go anywhere that could lead you into danger. Keep to wide well-lit streets where there are plenty of people. And find out which areas of town are no-go areas and avoid them.

Wherever you go, don't take more money than you need and keep it safe. Don't go out at night with people you don't know and when you do go out, go to places that are considered OK and know the names of those which are considered 'rough.'

Until you get to know your new city well, it is best not to go out alone at night. Arrange to go with friends to concerts, discos, films, sporting events, and restaurants and go home together. If possible, share a taxi. Never accept a lift from a stranger or someone you have only just met. And do not invite strangers to your home and do not go to theirs alone. It's quite common to feel lonely, and so it's a good idea to give yourself time to make friends through the various outings organized for overseas students at your college or university and gradually, you will become more independent and learn to find your way around more confidently. 'Look before you leap' is a good saying to remember here!

This may sound like a long list of don'ts but we want your stay here to be trouble-free and we are sure that if you observe a few precautions it will be! Well it only remains for me to say 'Take care! Enjoy yourselves and make the most of your time here!' Now, if there are any questions, I'll, er …

That is the end of Listening Test 3.

SPEAKING TEST 1
STEVE AND MARIA
Phase 1

S. Hello Maria.

M. Hello Steve.

S. Er. Could I have a look at your personal details?

M. Yeah. Sure.

S. Thanks. Right. Now... and you come from Malaysia?

M. Yeah. That's right.

S. Which part do you come from?

M. Um. East Coast. I'm from East Coast which is Terranganu Island. Yeah. It's in the East Coast of Peninsular Malaysia.

S. Right. Very nice. Is it very sunny?

M. Yeah. It's very sunny. It's hot and it's bright, clear. Sometimes it rains, get flooded. Yeah.

S. Uhuh. Do you er do you have any brothers or sisters?

M. Er yes. I have... how many? Let me think... I got er 5 sisters and 3 brothers.

S. Five? And are you the eldest?

M. Er no. I'm the 3rd.

S. The third?

M. Yeah.

S. And are some of them studying in Australia as well?

M. No. I'm... I'm the first... come here from my siblings. I'm the pioneer then.

S. Pioneer. Very good.

M. Yeah.

Phase 2

S. And er it says here that you're hoping to get into Medicine at university?

M. Yes.

S. OK. Um tell me a little bit about what happens when you're ill in Malaysia?

M. When I'm ill?

S. What happens when somebody's sick at home?

M. When somebody sick... yeah. Um. It just that um when a person is very sick, we usually send this person to the hospital.

S. Mm.

M. And if they're not really serious then you just... you know... stay at home... they can recover after that usually they can recover but if the sickness continue then we send this person to the hospital.

S. Right. Do you have er general practitioners, doctors who come and visit homes?

M. Er. No. I don't think so. No. No.

S. No. And what sort of um illnesses are er common in Malaysia... what do people often complain about er being sick, being off work or?

M. Nowadays I think common diseases common sickness do you mean... mm are fever, cold, sometimes cancer...yeah. Appendix.

S. And are the colds that you get in Malaysia similar to the colds you get in Australia?

M. Ah. I cannot. I don't know the difference 'cos I haven't got the common cold... but I think it's the same thing. Yeah.

S. Um. Tell me a little bit about the nearest hospital to Terranganu?

M. The nearest hospital? Ah. I don't know the exact distance but it takes about... let me see... 15 minutes to get to the hospital. That's the General Hospital. Yeah.

S. Uhuh. Is that is it a big hospital?

M. Yeah. It's a big hospital. Yeah.

S. What sort of departments does it have? Do you know?

M. Er... it's very rare for me to go hospital... very rare for me... sometimes... I'm not sure. I think... Children's Department... um... what else? I think it's the same like we have in Australia.

S. Right.

M. Yeah. TB. Tuberculosis... yeah. I'm not sure.

S. Uhuh. And er and er what do you do in Malaysia when you want an ambulance? Do you have a special number you can ring?

M. Yeah. I think so. Yeah... because er... I never called an ambulance before... so I think... yeah... we call this particular number to get a ambulance... it will come... it will come to our house usually I think. Yeah.

S. Uhuh. When, when did you first start to get interested in in er Medicine as a field of study?

M. In Matric 2. Matriculation 2.

S. Was there someone in you family who er encouraged you or was it just your own idea?

M. It's my elder sister actually. Yeah. She encouraged me a lot to pursue in Medicine.

S. Right er is she er involved in Medicine in some way?

M. She's not. She's teaching. Yeah.

S. So what er what appealed to you about er Medicine as a career ?

M. I think maybe the.... yeah it's not really wise to answer this but maybe because of the glamour I think.

S. The glamour?

M. Yeah, yeah, yeah. Because people are so... I mean when you tell people... you know... that you are doctor... they sort of you know respect... I'm not looking for that actually, actually I want to serve poor people... yeah.

S. But it's certainly an er an occupation that's well respected in Malaysia?

M. Yeah. Well respected. Yeah. Yeah.

Phase 3

S. OK, well er in the next stage of the interview Maria er I want you to ask me some questions.

M. OK.

S. So er er the idea is for you to find out some things about a weekend camp that's being organised for new students. So have a little look at that role play card and find out some information from me about the camp. I, I know one or two things about it. So when you're ready... just ask me some questions .

M. Alright.
Pause 15 seconds.

M. Ah Steve. May I know the purpose of the camp?

S. Yes,well we decided to er to have these camps some years ago because we think it's a good way for students to get to know each other in an informal way before their courses start so er it's a sort of getting to know you type camp .

M. Right. So where is being held held?

S. Er the camp is at a beach about 50 kilometres away from the University it's it's sort of south of the University, along the coast.

M. Ah. I see. So we're goin to camp at the beach. Near the seaside?

S. Yeah yeah near the seaside.

M. So. How about the arrangements for getting there and back?

S. Well er there'll be a bus which will pick up er students from the University and return er people to the same spot at the end of the camp so there's no problem with transport.

M. Right. So we're going there by bus?

S. Yeah it's a well a comfortable bus... the University bus.

M. Ah. I think it's enjoyable.

S. I think so.

M. Er may I know the cost? Do we have to pay a lot for it?

S. Er I'm afraid there is a cost yes but it's not too bad. It's $65 for the whole er stay and that includes all meals and all transport so er it's a long weekend Friday till Monday and all meals are included so that's very cheap.

M. Oh. Yeah. I think it's reasonable.

S. So are you interested in going?

M. Yeah. I think so.

S. I hope you do.

M. Yeah

Phase 4

S. OK. Let's er let's get back to thinking a little bit about er your future. Er we know that you want to er to study Medicine but er have you any thoughts about what sort of Medicine you're going to specialize in at the end of your studies?

M. Um. Let me think. I haven't decided yet. Yeah. But I have something in my mind. I think I want to continue for gynaecologist yeah...

S. Right.

M. ... but some friends... yeah... my friends sometimes... yeah... my friend told me that it's quite difficult for women... because Gynaecology's obstetrician, is it see... I'm not very sure... but yeah. So um... because it's quite pressure for woman and stressful I think because sometimes woman is not very good in handling pressure situation... yeah. I think I...

S. Oh right. Do you agree with that?

M. Yeah. Er in my case I think I agree because yeah... my friends... some of them are cool enough to handle the situation but I don't think I can do it.

S. What sort of pressure do you imagine er er it would involve?

M. Because... I don't know much about this field actually. Um well I know 'cos I watched a movie about this obstetrician and she... this person... this doctor... and she's she's going to deliver a baby. So it's quite stressful. I can see the situation... so... pathic er panic... so sometimes I think that I cannot handle it... so but I wish I can... 'cos it's a woman's job I think to to deliver a baby. Yeah.

S. Well I was going to say that er er in some ways one could argue that maybe it's er more suited to er a woman than a man?

M. Yeah. More suited to a woman yeah.

S. Many midwives are are women in a lot of countries. Do you have midwives in in Malaysia?

M. Yeah. We have a lot of midwives. Yeah.

S. And and do they deliver many of the babies? Or is it mainly doctors in hospitals?

M. I think er nowadays people prefer to go to the hospital so the doctor deliver the baby usually.

S. Right. Is there any any reason for that particularly?

M. Um. I don't know. I'm not sure about it. Maybe maybe because some parents... some some mothers think that it's safer. Yeah.

S. Right.

M. That doctors know more about delivering baby because er the midwife... er they're not very educated... it's just that they gain experience. Yeah.

S. I see. So they don't have a long training?

M. Oh yeah. Yeah. Yeah.

S. So do you agree with that view? Do you think er doctors do know more about...?

M. No. No. I'm not agree with that yeah er I think midwives are sometimes are better than doctors. Yeah.

S. It's difficult to generalize, isn't it?

M. Yeah.

S. So do you think there's a a big need for er doctors who are specialists in infant care or delivering babies in er Malaysia? Is that a growing area of need?

M. Yeah. It's a growing area. Yeah.

S. Is is there a a fast growing population in Malaysia do you know?

M. Um. You mean um growth of population?

S. Yeah.

M. Yeah. We have... yeah. Quite fast. The growth of population right yeah. The rate of... what you call that... the rate of birth?

S. The birth rate.

M. Yeah the birth rate is going up. Yeah.

S. Aha. So it could be a very important area for your country if you choose that?

M. Yes. Yes. Yes. Nowadays. Yes.

S. Well, perhaps at the end of your studies you'll be more confident because you'll have learnt so much more? Is that possible do you think?

M. Yeah. I hope so. I hope to gain more confident. That's why I come here.

Phase 5

S. Well I'd like to thank you Maria for er taking part er in the interview and wish you the best of luck with your studies.

M. Thank you Steve. Thank you very much. Yeah.

S. OK. It was nice to talk to you.

M. It was nice to talk to you too.

That's the end of phase 5 and the end of the interview.

SPEAKING TEST 2
WANDA AND PEHR
Phases 1 and 2

W. Hi, Pehr. How are you?

P. I'm fine, thank you.

W. Good. Um I see from your CV that you're from Sweden?

P. Yeah.. That's right. From Europe from Sweden. Yes.

W. Mm. And er I guess you've been studying English for a while now?

P. Yes. Do you mean here in Australia or before?

W. How long have you been studying English, all told?

P. Well, I've been study since I was er 10 years old maybe, partly in the primary and later on in secondary school in Sweden, yes.

W. Mm. Uh. Mm. Uh. And um is this your first er trip abroad?

P. This is my first trip trip to Australia. Yes, it is.

W. Mm. Mm. And where else have you travelled?

P. Well I haven't been in other places in Australia but later on I think I will go to other cities, yes.

W. Where do you think you might go in Australia?

P. Well, I'm for Christmas later on I'm invited to Brisbane to the Gold Coast as well, so I think I will pop up there for a while.

W. Mm. Great. Yes. The Gold Coast is a lot of fun. Although I don't know whether December's a very good time of the year in terms of the weather. I think it's a er it's very humid then.

P. Very humid and very warm. Yes, that's right yes.

W. Do you think you could cope with that?

P. I think I can stay inside and if I go out go out I have to go to the beach... instead I'll take a bath... take a swim.

W. Of course. That's the best way to get cool isn't it. Um. Also here on your CV you've mentioned that you're pretty much an outdoors type. You like downhill skiing for instance.

P. Yes, I do. I think I will do that later on when I come to Europe this winter.

W. Can you tell me something about er some of the uh the experiences you've had while you have been er skiing?

P. Some particularly...

W. Yeah. Memorable occasions.

P. ... memorable occasions? Yeah, last year in fact I was there just before the Olympic Games when I was visiting the Val d'Isere slopes. Very nice area. Scary slopes. Somewhere it's built very steep.

W. Why are they scary?

P. Well, they're very steep and icy. Of course that's exciting as well at the same time.

W. And er this is a... probably not a very good er question but have you had any um accidents while you've been skiing?

P. No not really. I just hurt my tum (thumb) some years ago. That can create a lot of problems because you use your hands and arms a lot when you ski. So...

W. Right. Oh yes yes. Um. I think er people who are novices... who begin to learn to ski... sometimes they er damage their legs and you see people coming back from holidays with their legs in plaster.

P. Yes Right.

W. Have you ever experienced em have you been any where where this has happened?

P. Yeah. I've seen a a a woman once, for a couple of years ago who broked her leg and you could see her bone sticking out from the flesh. It's quite...

W. Oh goodness.

P. Yes. It's not so funny.

W. Yes. That's quite gruesome isn't it.

P. Yes it is.

W. So it's quite dangerous .

P. Yeah. Yes you have to be careful and don't do stupid things. Yes, that's right.

W. Mm. And um windsurfing... now we're looking at er a different er climate here aren't we. One's a winter sport and the other's... Would you go windsurfing in the winter? Perhaps in Australia?

P. Perhaps in Australia. Yes that's right. But I think it's very important to have something to do during the summer and something to do at winter during the winter.

W. And um your um interest in windsurfing... Have you been involved in windsurfing for a long time?

P. Yes for 6 years I was competing er before and I'm looking forward because in a couple of days I will go down to Victor Harbor further down for some wind surfing I hope.

W. Oh. Right. So er you said you were competing. In what context?

P. Well. I was it was a er the in in just in Sweden National League in funboard and waveriding.

W. And did you have er many um good results?

P. No, I just was an average person who just love it for fun.

W. So this is something that you probably would enjoy doing in Australia too I imagine?

P. Yes. Yes. Especially with this weather coming now and during the summer, I would like... looking forward to that.

W. Yeah. It can get quite warm.

P. Yeah.

Phase 3

W. Okay. I would like to change the um conversation a little bit now and um I would like you, in this part to ask me questions. And I'm going to give you a piece of paper with some information on it and I would like you to take some time to read it and then when you've finished let me know and we'll start this section of the interview.
Pause 10 seconds.

W. Now in this part of the interview I would like you to ask me as many questions as you possibly can related to these topics and I would like you to ask me different types of questions. Now I would like you to imagine that you're new at the university and you have just found some cheap accommodation. Now, I'm the accommodation officer...

P. At the university?

W. That's right. And I can assist you with getting some inexpensive furniture. So if you would like to ask me some questions related to that topic?

P. Well, can you help me please?

W. Sure.

P. Well, it's like that I have found cheap accommodation here in the last day in the newspaper and er it's a one bedroom flat and but it's unfurnished so I want some advice how I could find some cheap furniture because I'm a student and I don't have so much money as you.

W. OK. Well yes. OK. Um you can either rent your furniture... it depends on... How long are you staying here?

P. Well I think it would be a year, I think, say, yes.

W. A year. Well you can either rent some pieces of furniture or perhaps better still, you can buy furniture.

P. So it's not so big difference between renting or buying from if I'm here for a year.

W. Mm. I think the long term rental of furniture could be quite costly.

P. So it's possible to to sell them later on to another student.

W. Yes. Yes. Yes. You can.

P. Great. Where do you think I can find some cheap used furniture then for a student?

W. So you want used furniture did you say?

P. No. Yes. Preferably, yes.

W. OK. So second hand furniture.

P. Yeah. From other students maybe?

W. Yes. And I also can recommend a warehouse that deals with second hand furniture of good quality.

P. Here. In Adelaide?

W. Yes. Our students often go there to buy second hand furniture.

P. OK. Good. Um and um, what do you think? Is there is there any possibility to use desks here in er at the university? Or do you think I have to buy a desk as well?

W. I think most students find it's very useful to have a desk at home.

P. If you want to study, yes. Maybe.

W. Yes. I think if you want to study it's probably very good.

P. OK. OK. Thank you very much.

Phases 4 and 5

W. All right. Great. Thank you. Now let's return to what we were talking about earlier on... and I asked you a little about your background... but primarily I asked about sport. I would like to ask you about your educational background and particularly, your studies. Can you tell me something about your university studies.

P. Yes. I'm... after my high school, secondary school in Sweden, I went to the university—University of Lund. It's in the southern part of Sweden in a part called Scania. Quite near Denmark and Germany...

W. Oh right.

P. ... and er I studied majorly Business Administration, Economics and Commercial Law at university for a half year.

W. Oh right. So um private business I suppose is the area that you would be most interested in?

P. Yeah. That's right. But, the the recession lately, in Europe especially have created a a condition there the most of the movements and the interesting thing is sometimes in the public sector.

W. Oh right.

P. So therefore maybe there'll be another possibilities there instead cause it's quite downgoing or in the private sector. Yes.

W. So does that mean that um unemployment is er high in Sweden at the moment?

P. Yes in fact when you hear the word Sweden you sometimes connect it with low unemployment figures but in fact today we have had quite high unemployment especially among young people and academic people yes.

W. I see. So the recession has hit the er ordinary Swede fairly harshly?

P. Yeah, that's right.

W. Mm. Um. One thing about Sweden that I've always well um believed is that there is a particularly high taxation rate. Is that true?

P. Yes, but since 2 or 3 years ago that had been changed not only the income taxation, also for example for taxation on alcohol...

W. Right.

P. ... and just to move the country much more towards the EC [1] 'cos we are had in EC plan enrolment for a couple of years ago...

W. Right.

P. ... so we intend to be a part of the EC in '95, yes.

W. Right. I don't know if you're aware but in Australia people are constantly complaining about our high taxation rate I don't think it's quite as high as Sweden's. What do people think about taxation in Sweden?

P. Generally. Well as most people as you said hate the word tax. It's not so funny when the tax bill comes. Um, but in fact I will I'm not really er agree with you about that because I think Sweden have the lower taxes now than Australia in fact. Especially when you, if you have, a, in a higher level of wages.

W. Oh right. What is the rate in Sweden?

P. Well. It's not no... it's not over 50%. It had been 80%.

W. 80%!

P. Quite often quite often it's just 35 or 30%. Which I think is quite alright.

W. Right. Mm. I'm not really aware of how much it is in Australia but I thought it was something like 39 or 40 %.

P. Well okay.

W. I think so. I'm not really sure. I'm not an economist.

P. Well okay. It depends if you talk about median or average figures it's working pretty good.

W. Mm. Mm. Yeah. But just going back to what you've just said about the recession... there seems to be quite a few countries in the world at the moment... Japan for instance, that are experiencing a bit of a downturn in the economy. Do you foresee any improvement in terms of the recession through out the globe? Do do you see that?

P. Yes. I see in in some parts, there of course if you look at these trade areas as the European market...

W. Right.

P. ... and recently we have heard about the the the er, agreement in America...

W. Right.

P. ... and some people in Australia for example don't understand that this would made it a little bit harder for Australian companies to export to these areas in America because there will be a trade war.

W. Yes.

P. But the important thing is not only the facts always, sometimes it's the expectations. So, I see some expectation in the world today, yes even if we have especially in Europe... we have some wars there as you know in the Eastern Europe and that's affect the whole economy but the expectation is much more important than the effects.

W. Yeah. I'm not quite clear what you mean by expectations. Can you?

P. Expectations... if you today if you have seen the statements and comments in the newspaper about this agreement in the...

W. Yes.

P. ... in America you see that most people are quite positive even if they know that it will in some cases hit Australia in a bad way.

W. This is um NAFTA [2].

P. NAFTA. Yes. Right. And. But the the dynamic effects are are forecast or expected to be more important than these smaller effects on special businesses in Australia and throughout the world. So... right

W. So. There'll be long term gains.

P. Right long term gains and with it big big communities, like, or big areas with free trade, will create a high competition, and then more movement of people and better allocation of resources.

W. Right. Well that sounds as if um there could be some improvement there.

P. We would hope so. Yes.

W. I think Australians are waiting for an

improvement in our economy as well.

P.   You've hit the recession. One of the first countries who hit the recession and that have been with us a long time. Stucked because you have had other your business partners have hit the recession later on. So you have had been hit a little bit harder than we have had. That's right.

W.   Yes. That's a shame isn't it. Oh well, we hope, I hope we can all come out of this safely and er we all do well in the end. Okay. Thank you very much. It was nice talking to you.

P.   Thank you.

W.   Good

That's the end of Phases 4 and 5 and the end of the interview.

[1] EC—European Community (now the European Union)

[2] NAFTA—North American Free Trade Agreement.

ANSWER KEY

LISTENING TESTS

* For some questions alternative answers are possible. This is shown by ‖

1

1. 40
2. student(s)
3. 2 hours
4. 8–10, 9–5
5. resource card
6. scanner
7. 95102975
8. name & (ID)number
9. eating & drinking
10. A
11. A & C
12. B
13. D
14. C
15. C
16. 70
17. T
18. F
19. F
20. N
21. F
22. T
23. F
24. C
25. (Barbara) SANCHEZ
26. Ms
27. 17a John (Street)
28. 5035
29. 3320578
30. afternoon‖pm
31. C
32. D & E
33. Seat belts‖Speed
34. Speed‖Seat belts
35. light truck(s)
36. 20 (%)
37. 42 (kph)
38. 0 (%)
39. 100 (kph)
40. B & D

2

1. 2 hours
2. B
3. Deep Harbour
4. D
5. adventure‖horror
6. horror‖adventure
7. URSINI
8. 65 Baron Road
9. 8590
10. 9211067
11. (Thurs) Feb 1‖1/2
12. (Tues) Feb 6‖6/2
13. 1983
14. $4.15
15. Grape Growing
16. $30
17. 4th
18. $13
19. latest‖2nd
20. fair
21. B
22. computer paper/ photocopy paper/old exam papers (any 2)
23. wrapping paper/ envelopes/paper bags (any 2)
24. B
25. reused
26. recycled
27. ripped
28. small pieces
29. coloured
30. manilla folders
31. trend
32. D
33. C
34. D
35. (very) expensive
36. outmoded
37. within companies
38. smaller companies & universities
39. B
40. A

3

1. B
2. A
3. D
4. C
5. O'Riordan
6. 30
7. Marryatville
8. MY679043
9. Between 8.40 and 9.10
10. 504
11. Transport authority
12. Library books & notes
13. rights
14. customs
15. food
16. tobacco‖alcohol‖firearms‖ drugs‖perfume
17. tobacco‖alcohol‖firearms‖ drugs‖perfume
18. fruit
19. car‖road‖plane‖air
20. plane‖air‖car‖road
21. signs
22. crops
23. (Vietnamese) sweets‖pork
24. (customs) declaration
25. no
26. spoken English‖Australian accent
27. no
28. his mother
29. (give) help (him)‖provide comfort
30. to lock up‖lock the doors & windows‖lock everything.
31. money‖valuables
32. lots of money
33. handbag‖wallet
34. unlocked
35. wide‖well-lit‖busy streets
36. you know‖who are known to you
37. with friends
38. a stranger's car‖a car with a stranger

If you have more than 25 answers correct on each test, you probably could achieve a score of 6.0 on the IELTS test.

READING TESTS

1	2	3

1

1. F
2. F
3. T
4. NI
5. F
6. B
7. B
8. B‖A
9. G
10. vii
11. iii
12. vi
13. ix
14. ii
15. G
16. H
17. I
18. E
19. A
20. C
21. C
22. D
23. B & C & E (in any order)
24. NI
25. T
26. F
27. T
28. F
29. B
30. E
31. F
32. G
33. cleaner industrial production
34. economic prosperity
35. environmental effects
36. 4
37. 7
38. 1
39. 8
40. 6

* Answers to questions 29–32 can be in any order.

2

1. F
2. NI
3. F
4. V
5. P
6. P
7. N
8. V
9. cognitive
10. pushing
11. skills
12. achieving
13. success
14. goals
15. C
16. I
17. B
18. A
19. NI
20. T
21. F
22. F
23. F
24. G
25. D
26. B
27. F
28. T
29. NI
30. F
31. E
32. B
33. A
34. H
35. D
36. G
37. level
38. pulley
39. diameter
40. inside
41. grip
42. skill
43. weight

2PB
292891

3

1. E
2. H
3. G
4. D
5. yin & yang‖blood & breath
6. physical & mental
7. age & pregnancy
8. intrinsic nature
9. physical effects
10. tonic
11. increase blood volume‖ (promote) health and energy
12. antitonic
13. sour food‖raw food‖cold food
14. wind illness‖rheumatism‖ arthritis
15. toxic
16. convulsions‖skin irritation‖infection
17. magic
18. 289‖>200 (not 200)
19. 5500–6500 miles
20. 5000 miles‖8000 km
21. 2.0 Mach
22. 2.4 Mach
23. 90m
24. C
25. H
26. F
27. B
28. 7
29. privacy & ownership
30. isolation
31. sharing/community/access (any 2)
32. (lack) privacy
33. C
34. D
35. F
36. household
37. dwelling
38. hobbies
39. music
40. residents

* Answers to questions 24–27 can be in any order.

If you have more than 25 answers correct on each test, you probably could achieve a score of 6.0 on the IELTS test.

READING TESTS

4	5	6
1. Sunday	1. language	1. community‖society
2. F	2. host(s)	2. support
3. IE	3. climate	3. homelike
4. F	4. anguish	4. F
5. IE	5. F	5. T
6. iii	6. F	6. F
7. v	7. IE	7. IE
8. vii	8. F	8. F
9. ii	9. IE	9. encephalitis‖accidents
10. i	10. T	10. accidents‖encephalitis
11. ix	11. (gift) giving	11. v
12. viii	12. pig	12. vi
13. vi	13. colours	13. ii
14. iv	14. black	14. vii
15. B	15. quality	15. (many) experts
16. E	16. weakness	16. pollutants
17. G	17. shell	17. batteries
18. E	18. shattering	18. 55%
19. A	19. human	19. 1937
20. F	20. earthquake	20. Yes
21. C	21. artificial	21. No
22. D	22. water	22. No
23. E	23. C	23. Not Given
24. M	24. A	24. Not Given
25. F	25. D	25. communication
26. I	26. vii	26. telephone
27. C	27. x	27. civilised
28. A	28. i	28. weather‖climate
29. C	29. xii	29. November
30. D	30. xi	30. D
31. A	31. viii	31. B
32. C	32. ii	32. A
33. I	33. v	33. C
34. G	34. & 35. city expansion‖	34. C
35. A	building roads‖salinity‖	35. E
36. world	alkalinity (any 2)	36. A
37. coral(s)	36. B	37. D
38. rain‖rainfall	37. D	38. humour
39. crown-of-thorns starfish	38. E	39. Avomine
40. ranger(s)	39. A	40. interview
	40. D	

If you have more than 25 answers correct on each test, you probably could achieve a score of 6.0 on the IELTS test.

READING TESTS

* For some questions alternative answers are possible. This is shown by ||

7

1. thin copper wires
2. reliable||highly accessible
3. & 4.
    (inexpensive)VT equipment||increased bandwidth||affordable cost (any 2)
5. F
6. T
7. T
8. IE
9. F
10. T
11. P
12. P
13. P
14. F
15. vii
16. iv
17. ii
18. vi
19. i
20. DL
21. OC
22. DL
23. OC
24. DL
25. DL
26. BM
27. BM
28. threat to democracy
29. more than one job
30. depersonalised screen
31. F
32. D
33. B
34. H
35. C
36. N
37. Y
38. N
39. N

8

1. W
2. C
3. W
4. W
5. B
6. environmental impact
7. superficial greening
8. research||design||materials|| technology
9. eco-design||life-cycle analysis||environmental design
10. environmental design
11. (the) environmental implications (of a product)
12. B
13. A
14. D
15. C
16. D
17. C
18. B
19. N
20. Y
21. Y
22. N
23. N
24. G
25. C
26. E
27. B
28. F
29. A
30. D
31. C
32. B
33. B
34. Y
35. Y
36. Y
37. N
38. Y
39. N
40. N
41. Y

9

1. social
2. demographic
3. man||woman living alone
4. will look abroad
5. C
6. C
7. E
8. E
9. A||B
10. Y
11. N
12. N
13. Y
14. N
15. T
16. T
17. F
18. T
19. H
20. C
21. E
22. D
23. B
24. G
25. F
26. Jasmine
27. ASET
28. archaeological
29. civilization
30. implements
31. skeletons
32. population
33. inhabitants
34. across
35. period
36. link
37. habitable
38. E
39. D
40. A
41. C
42. B

If you have more than 25 answers correct on each test, you probably could achieve a score of 6.0 on the IELTS test.

SPEAKING TESTS

	1		2
Phase 2A i.	a, b, c, e, f	Phases 4 & 5 A.	studies
Phase 2A ii.	9, 11, 13, 15, 17, 18, 20		recession
			trade
			university
			unemployment
			taxation
Maria's score.	probably low 6.0	Pehr's score.	about 7.0

SOURCES

Bell, A. 1989. Burning to save lives. *ECOS*. 59: 4–9. East Melbourne, Vic. CSIRO.

Brinkworth, J. 1995. Earthquakes: the shocking truth. *The Advertiser*. February 14: 33. Adelaide, SA. Advertiser Newspapers Limited.

Carver, S. and D. Lasscock. 1994. *Co-housing*. Adelaide, SA. The Halifax Eco-City Project.

Crase, J. 1994. The problems of mature job seekers. *The European*. October 14–20: 23. London, UK. The European Limited.

Cribb, J. G'day, is anyone out there? *The Australian Magazine*. April 29–30: 32–35. Canberra, ACT. Nationwide News Pty. Ltd. With permission from the author.

Cribb, J. 1992. Why we can't afford to let Asia starve. Reproduced from Rich World Poor World, *Issues for the Nineties*. 8: 33–34. Wentworth Falls, NSW. The Spinney Press. With permission from the author.

Da Silva, W. 1993. From the outback to the new frontier (graphic). *21•C the magazine of the 21st century*. Autumn: 11. Melbourne, Vic. Ashley Crawford.

Dunstan, S. 1994. Tools for tomorrow's telecommunications. *21•C the magazine of the 21st century*. Autumn: 56. Melbourne, Vic. Ashley Crawford.

Faulkner, R. 1992. Human powered pumps for African farmers. *Research report*. Armidale, NSW. University of New England.

Figgis, J. 1994. How to raise a bright child. *The Independent Monthly*. September: 58–59. Surry Hills, NSW. I. M. Publishing.

Franklin, C. 1994. Warning: Mondays are bad for your heart. *Elan. The European*. August 12–18: 16. London, UK. The European Limited.

Garet, F. 1995. Job equality 475 years off: ILO (graphic). *The Weekend Australian*. August 26–27: 16. Surry Hills, NSW. News Limited. With permission from Associated Press.

Kable, M. 1994. Passengers most at risk. *The Weekend Australian*. October 8–9: 12. Surry Hills, NSW. News Limited. With permission from the author.

Kestigian, M. 1994. Fuel cells: the 21st century's electricity generator. Reproduced from *Search: Science and Technology in Australia and New Zealand*. 25, 3: 94–96. Melbourne, Vic. Control Publications. With permission.

King, B. 1993. *Introduction to working as a distance educator*. 6–7. Adelaide, SA. University of South Australia.

Maiden, A. 1994. The hidden treasures of Aboriginal Australia. *The Independent Monthly*. September: 100–103. Surry Hills, NSW. I. M. Publishing.

Manderson, L. and M. Mathews. 1981. Traditional Vietnamese medical theory. Adapted from *The Medical Journal of Australia*. 1: 69–70. North Sydney, NSW. AMPCo. With permission.

Murphy, M. TV still at the heart of home life. Leisure at home (graphic). *The Advertiser*. June 24, 1995: 5. Adelaide, SA. Advertiser Newspapers Limited.

Neilson, R. 1993. Wrap up your visit with the perfect gift. *Lingo*. 2, 1: 6–8. Sydney, NSW. The Quay Connection.

NSW Council for Intellectual Disability. 1992. Intellectual Disability: Some Questions and Answers. *Issues for the nineties*. 15: 12. Wentworth Falls, NSW. The Spinney Press.

O'Neill, J. 1994. The value of driver training. *The Independent Monthly*. April: 64. Surry Hills, NSW. I. M. Publishing. With permission from the author.

Potter, M. 1995. The new supersonic boom. *The Advertiser*. March 16: 15. Adelaide, SA. Advertiser Newspapers Limited.

Roberts, G. 1994. Beautiful one day, wiped out the next. *The Bulletin*. September 13: 30–34. Sydney, NSW. ACP Publishing.

Rusek, W. 1994. *Domestic division of labour*. Adelaide, SA. With permission from the author.

Ryan, C. 1993. Reshaping desire. *21•C the magazine of the 21st century*. Autumn: 86–87. Melbourne, Vic. Ashley Crawford.

Short, D. 1994. A different taste of things to come. *The European*. October 14–20:21. London, UK. The European Limited.

Slater, S. 1995. *Self-Rating Guide for Writing Tasks*. Adelaide, SA. CALUSA

Smith, K., I. Smith and A. Thomas. 1992. Composting toilet. *The Australian Self-sufficiency Handbook*. 281. Ringwood, Vic. Penguin Books Australia.

Smith, R. 1994. The new ice age. *The Australian Way*. November: 36–42. Melbourne, Vic. David Symes and Co. Ltd.

Tagaza, E. 1994. New rules for the paper game. *ECOS*. 79: 14–17. East Melbourne, Vic. CSIRO.

The IELTS Handbook. 1995. Cambridge, UK. British Council, UCLES, IDP Australia.

Tranter, P. 1994. Finding the lost freedom. *Environment South Australia*. July/August 3,4: 6. Adelaide, SA. Conservation Council of SA Inc.

Van Aken, B. 1991. Rising seas. *ECOS*. 68: 6–9. East Melbourne, Vic. CSIRO.

Zinberg, D. 1994. Associations provide therapy for society. *The Australian*. October 12: 37. Surry Hills, NSW. News Limited . With permission from the author.

The authors are grateful for permission to use copyright material. Information that will enable the publisher to rectify any error or omission in subsequent editions will be welcome.